David Herbert has been obsessed with food since childhood.
Growing up in a small seaside town, his spare time was spent
fishing and thinking of new ways to cook his daily cat...

David is the author of *The Perfect Cookbook* and
contributes recipes to a weekly column in the *W...*
newspaper as well as numerous magazines both in...
and the UK. He is currently living and working in...
surrounded by his kitchen treasures, cookbooks
and copper saucepans.

more
perfect
recipes

more
perfect
recipes

David Herbert

photography by Andre Martin

LANTERN

an imprint of
PENGUIN BOOKS

LANTERN

Published by the Penguin Group
Penguin Group (Australia)
250 Camberwell Road, Camberwell, Victoria 3124, Australia
(a division of Pearson Australia Group Pty Ltd)
Penguin Group (USA) Inc.
375 Hudson Street, New York, New York 10014, USA
Penguin Group (Canada)
10 Alcorn Avenue, Toronto, Ontario, Canada M4V 3B2
(a division of Pearson Penguin Canada Inc.)
Penguin Books Ltd
80 Strand, London WC2R 0RL, England
Penguin Ireland
25 St Stephen's Green, Dublin 2, Ireland
(a division of Penguin Books Ltd)
Penguin Books India Pvt Ltd
11 Community Centre, Panchsheel Park, New Delhi – 110 017, India
Penguin Group (NZ)
Cnr Airborne and Rosedale Roads, Albany, Auckland, New Zealand
(a division of Pearson New Zealand Ltd)
Penguin Books (South Africa) (Pty) Ltd
24 Sturdee Avenue, Rosebank, Johannesburg 2196, South Africa

Penguin Books Ltd, Registered Offices: 80 Strand, London, WC2R 0RL, England

First published by Penguin Group (Australia), a division of Pearson Australia Group Pty Ltd, 2005

10 9 8 7 6 5 4 3 2 1

Text copyright © David Herbert 2005
Photographs copyright © Andre Martin 2005

'Slow-roasted Pork' from *Nigella Bites* by Nigella Lawson published by Chatto & Windus.
Used by permission of Random House Group Limited.

Cover and text design by Louise Leffler and Brad Maxwell © Penguin Group (Australia)
Photography by Andre Martin
Typeset in Meta, Garamond 3 and Bembo by Post Pre-press Group, Brisbane, Queensland
Printed and bound in China through Bookbuilders

National Library of Australia
Cataloguing-in-Publication data:

    Herbert, David (David John).
    More perfect recipes.

    Includes index.
    ISBN 1 920 98909 9.

    1. Cookery. I. Martin, Andre. II. Title.

    641.5

www.penguin.com.au

To my brother, Robert, with love

an a-z of perfect recipes

introduction.

More Perfect Recipes is a 'second helping' of my favourite foods. In this book you'll find over 120 delicious new recipes that I constantly cook and that reflect my approach to cooking – sometimes nostalgic, often eclectic and always easy to achieve.

I cannot remember a time when I didn't collect recipes, hoard cookbooks or dream up perfect dishes. My favorite recipes, altered and adjusted over time, have ended up in a series of handwritten notebooks – little books of souvenirs full of memories, dog-eared corners, crossings out and smudges of cake batter.

To write *More Perfect Recipes*, I turned, once again, to my notebooks for inspiration. And just as I did with the first *Perfect Cookbook*, I've tested and tested each recipe to make absolutely certain that it comes out perfect every time. These are my favourite dishes that have stood the test of time.

For me this book is a collection of versatile recipe ideas, all simple and easy to follow. Remember that cooking just takes a little confidence, a basic recipe and a keen appetite. The more you practice, the easier cooking becomes. Feel free to experiment with flavour variation and adjust the dishes to suit your own taste. I hope *More Perfect Recipes* will become a well-thumbed reference book in your kitchen.

affogato.

4 scoops good-quality vanilla ice-cream

50 ml (1³/₄ fl oz) Frangelico or amaretto
   liqueur

4 shots espresso coffee, freshly made

Place a scoop of ice-cream in each of four small glasses or demitasse (espresso cups). Drizzle an equal amount of the alcohol over each scoop of ice-cream and follow with the hot coffee. Serve immediately.

Serves 4

almond bread.

200 g (6½ oz) blanched almonds

5 egg whites

salt

200 g (6½ oz) caster (superfine) sugar

185 g (6 oz) plain (all-purpose) flour, sifted

Preheat the oven to 180°C (350°F, Gas Mark 4). Lightly grease a 23 × 11 × 8 cm (9 × 4½ × 3 in) loaf tin and line the base and two long sides with baking paper.

Spread the almonds on an oven tray and roast in the oven for 4–6 minutes, or until lightly toasted. Allow to cool.

Place the egg whites and a pinch of salt in a clean, dry bowl. Beat with an electric mixer on medium speed until stiff peaks form. (When you lift the mixer out of the bowl, the mixture should cling to the beaters, forming stiff and moist-looking peaks.) Add the sugar a little at a time, beating well after each addition. Beat until the mixture is stiff and glossy.

Gently fold the almonds and flour through the egg and sugar mixture with a large metal spoon. Spoon the mixture into the prepared tin and bake for 35–40 minutes, or until firm and lightly coloured. Remove from the oven and allow to cool in the tin.

Reduce the oven temperature to 140°C (275°F, Gas Mark 1).

Remove the almond bread from the tin and cut into 4 mm (⅙ in) slices using a serrated knife. Place slices in a single layer on two baking sheets and 'dry' in the preheated oven, turning once, for 10–15 minutes, or until crisp and lightly golden. Cool on a wire rack.

Serve with coffee or as an accompaniment to ice-cream. This almond bread can be stored in an airtight container for up to 2 weeks.

Makes 35 slices

apple and cinnamon teacake.

This is a great cake – the sliced apples, sugar and cinnamon cook together
to create a delicious topping.

1¹/₃ cups plain (all-purpose) flour

1 teaspoon baking powder

¹/₂ teaspoon salt

150 g (5 oz) unsalted butter, at room
 temperature

²/₃ cup caster (superfine) sugar

finely grated zest of 1 lemon

3 eggs

¹/₄ cup milk

2 Granny Smith apples

2 tablespoons demerara sugar or raw sugar

2 teaspoons ground cinnamon

Preheat the oven to 180°C (350°F, Gas Mark 4). Lightly grease a 23 cm (9 in) spring-form cake tin and line the base with baking paper.

Sift the flour, baking powder and salt into a bowl.

In a separate bowl, beat the butter, caster sugar and lemon zest with an electric mixer until fluffy, pale and well combined. Beat in the eggs one at a time, alternating with a little flour mixture, until all the eggs have been added. Fold in the remaining flour, then stir in the milk until the mixture is smooth. Spoon the batter into the prepared tin.

Peel, halve, core and thinly slice the apples and arrange on top of the cake, pressing down slightly. Combine the demerara sugar and cinnamon and sprinkle it over the apple.

Bake for 55–60 minutes, or until the cake feels firms to the touch and a skewer inserted into the centre comes out clean. Allow to cool in the tin for 10 minutes before removing and cooling on a wire rack.

apple tart.

This is my favourite kind of food – fast and simple (especially when made using ready-rolled puff pastry).

3 tablespoons apricot jam
1 sheet frozen puff pastry, thawed
2 dessert apples

2 tablespoons sugar
10 g ($^1/_4$ oz) butter

Preheat the oven to 200°C (400°F, Gas Mark 6). Add 2 tablespoons of hot water to the jam and stir until soft and spreadable.

Place the sheet of pastry on an oven tray lined with baking paper. Trim to make a 23 cm circle. Brush half the jam mixture over the pastry, leaving a 2 cm (¾ in) border all around.

Peel, halve and core the apples and cut each half into thin slices. Lay the slices, slightly overlapping, over the pastry, again leaving a 2 cm border all around.

Sprinkle the apples with the sugar and dot with the butter. Bake for 15–20 minutes, or until the pastry border is golden and its edges have risen.

Glaze the tart by brushing it with the remaining jam. Cut into quarters and serve hot or warm with cream or ice-cream.

Two peeled and thinly sliced ripe pears may be substituted for the apple. Ripe nectarines or large plums also make a delicious variation when in season. There is no need to peel them.

Serves 4

apricot turnovers.

1 quantity homemade flaky pastry (see
    page 122)
8 ripe apricots, halved, stoned and peeled
2 tablespoons demerara sugar or raw
    sugar, plus extra to decorate

1 teaspoon vanilla extract
25 g (1 oz) butter
1 egg, beaten

Prepare the pastry according to the instructions on page 122.

Divide the pastry into four equal portions. Roll each portion out to an 18 cm (7 in) square. Using a saucer as a guide, cut one 16 cm (6 in) diameter circle from each square.

Lightly grease an oven tray and transfer pastry circles to it.

Preheat the oven 200°C (400°F, Gas Mark 6).

Roughly chop the apricots and place a quarter of the fruit on one half of each pastry circle, leaving a 1 cm border. Sprinkle the sugar and vanilla equally over the piles of apricots, and dot each pile with a quarter of the butter.

Brush the edge of the pastry circle with a little of the beaten egg. Fold the pastry over the fruit to make a semicircle and seal the edge with a fork. Repeat with the remaining pastries.

Brush the turnovers with the remaining beaten egg and make 2 small slashes in the top of each. Sprinkle with a little extra sugar. Bake for 20 minutes, or until crisp and golden. Allow to cool on a wire rack for 5 minutes before eating. Serve with cream, crème fraîche or ice-cream.

Makes 4

asparagus.

The lovely, fresh flavour and vibrant colour of asparagus is a real treat during
spring and early summer, when this vegetable is at its best and cheapest.
I love it boiled, grilled or roasted.

The key to perfectly boiled asparagus is to cook it briefly. Bring a large saucepan of salted water to a rapid boil. Add 250 g (8 oz) – one large bunch – of fresh asparagus. Return to the boil (the stems will turn bright green) and cook for 2–3 minutes, or until tender when pierced with a skewer.

To grill asparagus, preheat a ribbed grill plate to very hot. Lightly brush the asparagus spears with olive oil and cook in a single layer for 4–6 minutes (this will depend on the thickness of the stalks), turning occasionally, or until tender and lightly browned.

To roast asparagus, arrange the stems in a single layer in a baking tin. Brush with a little olive oil and season with freshly ground black pepper. Roast in a preheated 200°C (400°F, Gas Mark 6) oven for 8–12 minutes, turning occasionally, or until tender. Serve hot or at room temperature.

When buying asparagus, look for stiff, bright-green stalks with smooth tips and freshly cut ends. Choose stems of similar thickness so that they will cook evenly.

To prepare asparagus, trim away any woody stems.

To store asparagus, wrap it in moist paper or cloth and keep it refrigerated. Eat it within 2 days.

Cooked asparagus is great dotted with a little lemon butter. It is also delicious simply dressed with olive oil, lemon juice, salt and freshly ground black pepper. Good matches for asparagus are eggs, butter, cheese, mayonnaise, lemon, pastry, goat's cheese, feta, mint, salmon and prawns. It also goes well with buttered brown bread.

asparagus risotto.

1.25 litres chicken stock or vegetable stock

1 × 250 g bunch asparagus, trimmed and
    cut into 3 cm lengths

40 g (1^1/$_2$ oz) butter

1 onion, finely chopped

1 cup Carnaroli or Vialone Nano rice

grated zest of 1 lemon

^{1}/$_2$ cup dry white wine

^{3}/$_4$ cup freshly grated parmesan

salt and freshly ground black pepper

Bring the stock to a simmer in a large saucepan. Add asparagus and cook for 2 minutes. Remove with a slotted spoon and set aside, leaving stock simmering.

Melt half the butter in a large saucepan over medium heat. Add the onion and sauté for 5 minutes, or until soft. Add the rice and lemon zest and cook, stirring gently, for 2 minutes. Add the wine. Stir and allow most of the liquid to evaporate.

Add enough of the simmering stock to just cover the rice. Stirring frequently, allow the rice to absorb most of the stock. Repeat the process, stirring well and adding stock as required. It will take 18–25 minutes to cook. Taste the rice for texture – it should be soft but still retain a little bite.

Remove from the heat and gently stir in the asparagus and parmesan. Season to taste with salt and freshly ground black pepper. Dot with the remaining butter, cover and rest for 5 minutes before serving.

Arborio rice can also be used to make risotto, but Carnaroli or Vialone Nano rice will produce a creamier result.

Serves 4

baked ricotta.

3 cups fresh ricotta

1 clove garlic, peeled and finely chopped

2 tablespoons chopped fresh herbs (chives, flat-leaf parsley and thyme are a good combination)

1 teaspoon grated lemon zest

1 teaspoon paprika, plus a little extra

salt and freshly ground black pepper

2 egg whites

extra-virgin olive oil, to drizzle

Place the ricotta in a fine sieve set over a bowl, and leave in a cool place to drain for 1–2 hours.

Preheat the oven to 180°C (350°F, Gas Mark 4). Grease a small loaf tin or 1-litre capacity ovenproof dish with vegetable oil and line the base with baking paper.

Place the drained ricotta in a bowl and stir in the garlic, herbs, lemon zest and the 1 teaspoon of paprika. Season to taste with salt and freshly ground black pepper.

Beat the egg whites in a clean, dry bowl until soft peaks just form. Gently fold a little of the egg whites through the ricotta mixture to slacken it, then carefully fold through the remaining whites.

Spoon the mixture into the prepared tin or dish and smooth the top. Sprinkle with a few extra pinches of paprika and drizzle with a little extra-virgin olive oil. Bake for 55–65 minutes, or until set, risen slightly and golden. Allow to cool in the tin before turning out to serve.

Baked ricotta is delicious spread on crusty bread or cut into pieces and served with roasted vegetables or with a tomato salad.

Serves 10 as part of antipasto or meze plate

banana smoothie.

1 ripe banana, roughly chopped
$^3/_4$ cup milk
$^1/_2$ cup plain natural yoghurt

1 tablespoon honey
4 ice cubes
pinch of grated nutmeg

Place the banana, milk, yoghurt, honey and ice cubes into a blender and pulse until smooth.

Divide the mixture between 2 large glasses. Garnish each smoothie with a pinch of nutmeg.

A few strawberries make a nice addition to a banana smoothie. And the milk can be replaced with freshly squeezed orange juice.

For a different flavour altogether, substitute the banana for a ripe mango or peach.

Makes 2

barbecue sauce.

1 tablespoon vegetable oil

1 onion, finely chopped

2 cloves garlic, crushed

1 teaspoon grated fresh ginger

1 cup tomato sauce (ketchup)

100 ml ($3^{1}/_{2}$ fl oz) red-wine vinegar

$^{1}/_{2}$ cup lightly packed brown sugar

2 teaspoons French-style mustard

2 tablespoons Worcestershire sauce

2 tablespoons lemon juice

1 teaspoon crushed chilli

$^{1}/_{2}$ teaspoon cayenne pepper

$^{1}/_{2}$ teaspoon salt

salt, extra, and freshly ground black pepper

Heat the oil in a frying pan over medium heat and cook the onion, garlic and ginger for 4–5 minutes, or until the onion is soft. Add all the remaining ingredients except the extra salt and freshly ground black pepper, and bring to the boil. Reduce the heat and simmer gently for 30 minutes, stirring occasionally, until the sauce has thickened. Season to taste with salt and freshly ground black pepper.

This sauce will keep for several weeks in an airtight jar in the refrigerator.

Makes 2 cups

beef and mushroom pie.

100 ml (3¹/₂ oz) olive oil

2 onions, sliced

2 cloves garlic, crushed

150 g (5 oz) button mushrooms, halved

¹/₃ cup plain (all-purpose) flour

1 kg (2 lb) rump or chuck steak, cut into
    5 cm (2 in) cubes

300 ml (9¹/₂ fl oz) beef stock or water

300 ml (9¹/₂ fl oz) red wine

4 sprigs thyme

2 bay leaves

2 teaspoons Worcestershire sauce

salt and freshly ground black pepper

1 quantity quick flaky pastry (see page 122)
    or 1 × 380 g (12 oz) packet frozen puff
    pastry, thawed

1 egg, beaten, to glaze

Preheat the oven to 180°C (350°F, Gas Mark 4). Heat 2 tablespoons of the oil in a large frying pan over medium heat. Add the onion, garlic and mushrooms and cook, stirring occasionally, for 7 minutes, or until tender. Transfer to a large saucepan or casserole dish.

Lightly dust the meat with the flour. Reserve 2 tablespoons of the flour.

Heat 2 tablespoons of the oil in the frying pan and cook the meat in batches over high heat, adding a little extra oil if needed, until browned. Transfer to the saucepan.

Sprinkle the frying pan with the reserved flour and cook, stirring, for 1 minute. Stir in the stock and wine and bring to the boil, then pour over the meat. Return the saucepan to the heat, add the thyme and bay leaves and bring to the boil. Cover, transfer to the oven and cook for 1½ hours, stirring occasionally. Stir in the Worcestershire sauce and season well with salt and pepper. Allow to cool – preferably chill overnight.

Preheat the oven to 190°C (375°F, Gas Mark 5).

Spoon the mixture into a large pie dish. Roll out the pastry to the size of the dish. Cover the pie, pressing down on the edges to seal. Trim away any excess pastry, brush with the beaten egg and bake for 40–45 minutes, or until the pastry is golden.

Serves 4

braised pork chops with apple.

4 **pork loin chops**	1 **cup dry cider or apple juice**
$^1/_3$ **cup plain (all-purpose) flour**	2 **cups chicken stock (approximately)**
$^1/_3$ **cup olive oil**	1 **large cooking apple, peeled and**
4 **rashers streaky bacon, diced**	**coarsely grated**
1 **large shallot, sliced**	4 **sprigs thyme**
2 **leeks, sliced**	1 **bay leaf**
2 **cloves garlic, crushed**	**salt and freshly ground black pepper**

Preheat the oven to 200°C (400°F, Gas Mark 6). Lightly dust the chops with the flour.

Heat 2 tablespoons of the oil in a large frying pan over medium heat and cook two chops at a time, until brown on both sides. Transfer to a large casserole dish. Repeat with the remaining chops, adding a little extra oil if needed.

Heat the remaining 2 tablespoons of oil in the frying pan over medium heat. Add the bacon and cook for 2 minutes. Add the shallot, leek and garlic and cook, stirring occasionally, for 6–7 minutes, or until the vegetables are tender but not coloured. Transfer to the casserole dish. Deglaze the pan with cider and pour over pork.

Stir into the casserole the stock (add enough to just cover the meat), apple, thyme and bay leaf and bring to the boil over medium heat. Cover, transfer to the oven and cook for 30 minutes. Reduce the heat to 170°C (330°F, Gas Mark 3) and cook for a further 45 minutes, or until tender. Turn the chops occasionally during cooking. Remove the lid about 30 minutes before the end of the cooking time.

Remove from the oven, skim off any fat and remove the bay leaf. Season well with salt and pepper and serve with boiled new potatoes and steamed green beans.

Serves 4

bruschetta.

Bruschetta are slices of toasted bread rubbed with garlic and drizzled with olive oil. They are classically (and best of all) served with lots of chopped ripe tomato, good-quality olive oil and freshly torn basil – a wonderfully simple and delicious snack.

4 × 1 cm ($^1/_2$ in) thick slices coarsely textured, crusty, Italian-style white bread	good-quality virgin olive oil
	3 large ripe Roma (egg) tomatoes
	fresh basil
1 clove garlic, peeled	sea salt and freshly ground black pepper

Toast the bread on both sides, or grill it on a ribbed chargrill pan. Rub the toasted slices lightly with the clove of garlic and drizzle each slice generously with olive oil.

Meanwhile, roughly chop the tomatoes and place in a bowl along with any juices. Add a few torn basil leaves and drizzle over a little olive oil. Season the tomato mixture well with sea salt and freshly ground black pepper.

Divide the tomato mixture between the slices of bread, spooning it generously over each slice. Serve immediately.

Use the best ripe tomatoes you can find – if possible, beg, borrow or steal some home-grown ones. As a variation, add some coarsely chopped rocket leaves to the tomato mix.

Other interesting bruschetta toppings include cooked onions, sautéed sliced mushrooms mixed with herbs and garlic, or fried diced eggplant (aubergine) dressed with oil, lemon juice and sprinkled with mint.

Serves 2

carrot salad.

$^1/_4$ cup olive oil	$^1/_3$ cup pine nuts
1 tablespoon lemon juice	4 large carrots, scrubbed
1 clove garlic, crushed	2 tablespoons chopped mint
salt and freshly ground black pepper	2 tablespoons chopped flat-leaf parsley

Combine the oil, lemon juice and garlic in a small screw-top jar. Season with salt and freshly ground black pepper.

Place the pine nuts in a dry frying pan over medium heat and toss for 5 minutes, or until toasted and golden. Set aside.

Finely grate the carrots into a bowl. Stir in the chopped herbs.

Shake the dressing until combined and remove the garlic. Drizzle enough dressing over the carrots to just coat them. Sprinkle with the pine nuts.

Use only the best quality carrots, preferably organic, for this dish.

I sometimes replace one of the carrots with a finely grated apple.

Serves 4

chicken cacciatore.

4 chicken thighs

4 chicken legs

salt and freshly ground black pepper

$1/4$ cup olive oil

150 g (5 oz) pancetta or bacon, roughly
    chopped

1 onion, chopped

2 sticks celery, thinly sliced

2 cloves garlic, crushed

100 ml ($3^1/2$ fl oz) white wine

2 × 400 g (13 oz) cans crushed or chopped
    tomatoes

2 bay leaves

3 sprigs thyme

Season the chicken pieces with salt and freshly ground black pepper. Heat 2 tablespoons of the oil in a large frying pan over high heat and fry the chicken a few pieces at a time until golden on each side. Transfer the chicken to a large saucepan.

Heat the remaining oil in the frying pan over medium heat. Add the pancetta and cook, stirring occasionally, for 2 minutes. Add the onion, celery and garlic and cook, stirring from time to time, for 6–8 minutes, or until the onion is tender. Transfer to the saucepan with the chicken.

Return the frying pan to the heat and deglaze with the white wine. Transfer to the saucepan and add the tomatoes with their juice, bay leaves and thyme. Bring to the boil over medium heat. Reduce the heat, cover and leave to simmer, turning chicken occasionally, for 25–30 minutes, or until the chicken is tender.

Check the sauce and add a little water if necessary. Alternatively, if the sauce is too thin, remove the chicken, increase the heat and cook until the sauce has reduced and thickened. Season to taste with salt and freshly ground black pepper and serve with boiled potatoes.

Serves 4

chicken casserole with peas and pancetta.

4 chicken breasts

4 chicken thighs with drumsticks attached

$^1/_3$ cup plain (all-purpose) flour

$^1/_3$ cup olive oil

150 g (5 oz) pancetta, cubed

12 very small onions, peeled

2 leeks, sliced

2 cloves garlic, crushed

2 cups white wine

2 cups chicken stock

1 bay leaf

250 g (8 oz) frozen peas, thawed

salt and freshly ground black pepper

2 tablespoons chopped flat-leaf parsley

Preheat the oven to 180°C (350°F, Gas Mark 4). Lightly dust chicken with the flour.

Heat half the oil in a large frying pan over medium heat. Season the chicken pieces and cook in batches, adding a little extra oil if needed, until browned. Be careful not to overcrowd the frying pan, as the meat will then steam rather than sear. Transfer to a large, heatproof casserole dish.

Heat the remaining oil in the frying pan over medium heat. Add the pancetta, onion, leek and garlic and cook, stirring occasionally, for 7–10 minutes, or until the vegetables are tender and the onion is lightly coloured. Transfer to the casserole dish.

Place the frying pan back over the heat and deglaze with the wine. Transfer to the casserole dish and stir in the bay leaf. Bring to the boil over medium heat. Cover, transfer to the oven and cook for 1 hour, stirring occasionally.

Stir in the peas, return to the oven and cook for a further 15 minutes. Season to taste with salt and freshly ground black pepper. Remove the bay leaf and stir in the parsley before serving.

Serves 4–6

chicken, lemon and rocket risotto.

1.25 litres (40 fl oz) chicken stock

3 skinless chicken breasts

50 g (1³/₄ oz) butter

1 onion, finely chopped

1 cup arborio or Vialone Nano rice

grated zest of 1 lemon

¹/₃ cup dry white wine

75 g (2¹/₂ oz) parmesan, freshly grated

50 g (1³/₄ oz) rocket (arugula), shredded

salt and freshly ground black pepper

Bring the stock to a gentle simmer in a large saucepan. Add the chicken breasts, return to simmering point and cook for about 10 minutes, or until the chicken is cooked through. Remove the meat, allow it to cool a little, then shred or chop and set aside until the risotto is cooked.

Meanwhile, heat 30 g (1 oz) of the butter in a large, heavy-based saucepan over medium heat. Add the onion and cook, stirring, for 5 minutes, or until soft but not coloured. Add the rice and lemon zest to the onion and stir gently for 2 minutes. Add the wine, stir and allow most of the liquid to evaporate.

Add enough of the simmering stock to just cover the rice. Stir and allow the rice to absorb most of the stock. Repeat the process, stirring well and adding stock as required. It will take 18–25 minutes to cook. Taste the rice for texture – it should be soft but still retain a little bite.

Remove from the heat and stir in the chicken meat, parmesan and rocket. Add the remaining butter, cover and rest for 5 minutes before serving. Season to taste with salt and freshly ground black pepper.

Serves 4

Riso Semifino
Vialone Nano
Riseria Veneta s.n.c.
☎ 049 9065122
Campodoro (PD)
PESO NETTO 1000 g ℮
da consumarsi preferibilmente entro il

chicken liver pâté.

Chicken liver pâté seems to have fallen out of fashion, and I can't understand why.
It is easy to make, can be made ahead of time and is really delicious.

250 g (8 oz) chicken livers

225 g (7 oz) butter

1 clove garlic, finely chopped

2 small brown shallots or half an onion,
    finely chopped

$^1/_2$ teaspoon fresh thyme leaves

2 tablespoons brandy

pinch of grated nutmeg

salt and freshly ground black pepper

50 g ($1^3/_4$ oz) butter, extra

Trim the chicken livers of any stringy or green bits. Rinse livers, then pat dry with kitchen paper.

Melt 20 g (¾ oz) of the butter in a large frying pan over medium heat. Add the garlic and shallots and cook, stirring, for about 5 minutes, or until softened. Add the livers and thyme and cook, stirring frequently, for about 3 minutes, or until the livers are coloured on the outside but pink in the centre. Pour in the brandy, cook for an extra 10 seconds, then transfer the mixture to an electric blender.

Meanwhile, dice the remaining butter and let it soften a little. Turn on the blender and add the diced butter bit by bit, until the mixture is really smooth. Add the nutmeg and season to taste with salt and freshly ground black pepper. Spoon the pâté into 4–6 ¾-cup capacity ramekins or one large terrine dish.

Melt the extra butter and pour a little over the pâté. Cover with plastic wrap and refrigerate for at least 12 hours before eating.

Remove the pâté from the fridge about 20 minutes prior to serving. Serve with crusty bread or hot toast with lashings of butter.

Serves 4–6

chicken pot roast.

This great all-in-one dish needs minimal attention once it's in the oven.

2 tablespoons vegetable oil

1 large chicken

2 rashers bacon, chopped

2 onions, peeled and quartered

4–6 large carrots, peeled and cut into
    5 cm (2 in) pieces

8–10 small potatoes, peeled and halved

1 leek, thickly sliced

salt and freshly ground black pepper

1 tablespoon plain (all-purpose) flour

1 cup white wine

300 ml (9^1/$_2$ fl oz) chicken stock

4 sprigs thyme

2 bay leaves

Preheat the oven to 180°C (350°F, Gas Mark 4).

Heat the oil in a large, heatproof casserole dish over medium heat. Add the chicken and brown on all sides. Remove and set aside.

Add the bacon, onion, carrot, potato and leek to the casserole dish. Cook over medium heat, stirring occasionally, for 5–10 minutes, or until slightly coloured. Season well with salt and freshly ground black pepper. Sprinkle over the flour and cook, stirring, for 1 minute. Pour in the wine and stir with a wooden spoon, scraping up any bits stuck to the bottom.

Return the chicken to the casserole and pour in the chicken stock to a depth of 1 cm (½ in). Tuck in the thyme and bay leaves. Cover tightly with foil or with a lid, place in the oven and roast for 1½ hours, basting occasionally with the pan juices. Remove the lid 20 minutes before the end of the cooking time to allow the chicken to brown.

Remove the chicken and vegetables to a warm dish and check the sauce. Skim off any fat, adjust the seasoning and, if the sauce is too thin, reduce it over high heat on the stove top. Pour the sauce over the chicken.

Serves 4

chilli oil.

Chilli oil is easy to make, and using it is a simple way to add a little spice to a dish. Use it in marinades or dressings, drizzle it on bread or a pizza or add a little when making a stir-fry.

2 cups olive oil or vegetable oil

4 large red chillies, roughly chopped

1 bay leaf

1 clove garlic, peeled

1 teaspoon cayenne pepper

Pour the oil into a saucepan and place over gentle heat. When the oil is hot but not simmering, add the chilli, bay leaf and garlic and stir in the cayenne pepper. Heat gently for 5 minutes.

Remove from the heat, cover the pan and set it aside to cool. Leave the oil to infuse for 4 hours.

Strain through a fine sieve (or through muslin if you have some) into a clean and sterilised bottle. Label and date the bottle.

I often add a large, fresh red chilli or two to the bottle before filling (pierce the chillies with a skewer to help them sink).

You can use either fresh or dried chillies for the oil. I use large, red, milder chillies, but add a few small hot ones if you like.

Use olive oil rather than vegetable oil if you want to give the chilli oil as a gift or use it for dressings.

Makes 2 cups

chilli sauce.

This recipe is an easy homemade version of sweet chilli sauce – great as an accompaniment to Asian-style chicken, fish or noodle dishes.

1 cup white-wine vinegar or rice vinegar

1 cup sugar

2 cloves garlic, finely chopped

3 large red chillies, finely chopped

1 × 1 cm ($^1/_2$ in) piece fresh ginger, grated

$^1/_2$ teaspoon salt

1 tablespoon fish sauce

Place the vinegar, sugar and ¾ cup of water in a saucepan. Bring to a boil over medium heat, stirring to dissolve the sugar. Add the garlic, chilli, ginger, salt and fish sauce. Reduce the heat and simmer for 25–30 minutes, or until the sauce has thickened and is syrupy.

Sterilise a 3-cup-capacity glass-lidded bottle or jar by filling it with boiling water. Drain on a clean tea towel.

Fill the jar with the hot sauce and seal. Store in the refrigerator for up to 1 month.

It's a good idea to always wear gloves when handling chilli.

Makes 2 cups

chinese-style braised chicken.

2 chicken breasts

4 chicken thighs with drumsticks attached

150 ml (4^1/$_2$ fl oz) soy sauce

200 ml (6^1/$_2$ fl oz) light soy sauce

^{1}/$_3$ cup dry sherry

2 whole star anise

2 cloves garlic, peeled

4 × 4 mm (^{1}/$_4$ in) slices fresh ginger

1 tablespoon sea salt

salt, extra, and freshly ground black pepper

2 teaspoons sesame oil

Place the chicken pieces in a large saucepan and add the soy sauces, sherry, star anise, garlic, ginger and salt and enough water to just cover the chicken. Bring slowly to the boil over low heat. Cover and simmer gently for 15 minutes. Turn the chicken pieces, replace the lid and simmer very gently for a further 15 minutes. Remove from the heat and leave the chicken in the covered saucepan for 20 minutes.

Remove the chicken from the saucepan, reserving the sauce, and pat dry with kitchen paper. Cut the breasts in half. Bring the sauce back to the boil and season to taste with salt and freshly ground black pepper.

Meanwhile, lightly brush the chicken with the sesame oil and grill under medium–high heat for 5–10 minutes, or until heated and crisp.

Serve the chicken pieces in individual bowls and pour over a little of the sauce. Offer a bowl of sauce on the side, as a dipping sauce, and accompany the meat with spinach or steamed Asian greens.

Serves 4

chocolate chip cookies.

125 g (4 oz) plain (all-purpose) flour

$^1/_2$ teaspoon bicarbonate of soda
   (sodium bicarbonate)

salt

125 g (4 oz) butter, softened

$^1/_2$ cup caster (superfine) sugar

1 teaspoon vanilla essence

1 large egg, lightly beaten

125 g (4 oz) dark chocolate chips

Preheat the oven to 180°C (350°F, Gas Mark 4). Line two oven trays with baking paper.

Sift the flour, bicarbonate of soda and a pinch of salt into a bowl.

In a separate bowl, beat the butter, sugar and vanilla essence with an electric mixer until fluffy, pale and well beaten. Beat in the egg, a little at a time, alternating with a little of the sifted flour mixture, until combined. Fold in the remaining flour, then stir in the chocolate chips until combined.

Using a tablespoon, scoop up walnut-sized pieces of dough and place them on the prepared oven trays, leaving room for each to spread a little. Bake for 8–10 minutes, or until the cookies are firm and coloured. You may need to bake a third tray if any mixture remains. Cool on a wire rack.

These cookies are also good with the addition of 50 g (1¾ oz) of chopped pecans.

Makes about 30

chocolate fondant puddings.

200 g (6½ oz) good-quality dark chocolate, chopped (luxury Belgian dark chocolate is ideal)
100 g (3½ oz) butter, chopped

3 eggs
2 egg yolks
100 g (3½ oz) caster (superfine) sugar
¼ cup plain (all-purpose) flour

Thickly butter and flour 4 × 200 ml (6½ fl oz) metal pudding tins. Place the tins in the freezer to chill while you make the mixture.

Melt the chocolate and butter in a heatproof bowl set over a small saucepan of barely simmering water, stirring occasionally, until smooth.

In an electric mixer, beat the eggs, egg yolks and sugar on medium speed for 3–4 minutes, or until thick and pale. Gradually add the chocolate mixture, mixing until combined. Sift in the flour and fold through until smooth.

Spoon the mixture into the prepared pudding tins, filling them almost to the top. Transfer to the refrigerator and chill for at least 30 minutes – the puddings can be made ahead of time and stored in the refrigerator for up to 24 hours.

Preheat the oven to 200°C (400°F, Gas Mark 6).

Bake for 11 minutes (the cooking time is crucial) and remove from the oven. The puddings should be set on the top. Allow them to sit in their tins for 2 minutes, then loosen the puddings by running a knife around the inside edge of the tins. Invert each tin onto a serving plate and serve with scoops of vanilla ice-cream.

The mixture can also be frozen (uncooked) in pudding moulds for up to 4 weeks. Frozen puddings will need to be cooked for 25 minutes from frozen.

Makes 4

chocolate macaroons.

3 large egg whites
³/₄ cup caster (superfine) sugar
100 g (3¹/₂ oz) ground almonds
  (almond meal)

¹/₄ cup cocoa, sifted
salt
1 teaspoon vanilla extract

Preheat the oven to 170°C (340°F, Gas Mark 3). Line two oven trays with baking paper.

Using an electric mixer, whisk the egg whites until fluffy, then gradually beat in ⅓ cup of the sugar, until the mixture is glossy and firm peaks form.

Combine the remaining sugar and the ground almonds, cocoa and a pinch salt, and gently fold into the egg whites with a large metal spoon, until thoroughly blended. Stir in the vanilla extract.

Drop tablespoonfuls of the mixture onto the prepared oven trays, leaving a little space between each for spreading. Bake for 15–20 minutes, or until the macaroons are firm but not dry. You may need to bake a third tray if any mixture remains. Allow to cool on the trays for 5 minutes before carefully transferring to a wire rack to cool completely. Store in an airtight container in a cool, dry place for up to 5 days.

Macaroons are wonderful sandwiched together with a little chocolate ganache. Melt 150 g (5 oz) of dark chocolate with 100 ml (3½ fl oz) of cream in a small saucepan over low heat, stirring until smooth. Chill, then beat well with a wooden spoon. Sandwich between macaroons and set aside for 2 hours before serving.

Makes about 36

chocolate muffins.

150 g (5 oz) dark chocolate, chopped

125 g (4 oz) butter, chopped

2 cups self-raising (self-rising) flour

1 teaspoon baking powder

4 tablespoons cocoa

salt

100 g (3¹/₂ oz) dark chocolate chips

1 cup caster (superfine) sugar

185 ml (6 fl oz) milk

1 teaspoon lemon juice

2 eggs

Preheat the oven to 180°C (350°F, Gas Mark 4). Grease a 12-cup muffin tin or line with paper patty cases.

Melt the chocolate and butter in a heatproof bowl set over a saucepan of barely simmering water, stirring occasionally, until smooth.

Sift the flour, baking powder, cocoa and a pinch of salt into a mixing bowl. Stir in the chocolate chips and sugar and make a well in the centre.

In a jug, combine the milk, lemon juice and eggs and pour into the well in the flour mixture. Pour in the melted chocolate and butter and stir until the ingredients are just combined. Do not over-mix – the batter should not be smooth.

Divide the mixture evenly between the muffin cups. Bake for 20 minutes, or until the muffins are firm to the touch. Allow to cool in the tin for 10 minutes, then turn out onto a wire rack to cool completely.

These muffins are good served warm and simply dusted with cocoa or icing (confectioners') sugar.

If you do want to ice them you can make chocolate icing by melting 200 g (6½ oz) of chopped dark chocolate in a bowl set over a saucepan of barely simmering water, stirring occasionally, until smooth. Stir in ½ cup of sour cream and ¼ cup of icing (confectioners') sugar and mix until smooth. Remove from the heat and spread over the muffins.

Makes 12

chocolate peanut butter cake.

Chocolate and peanut butter is the perfect combination for me – and this is a cake for the child in all of us. This recipe gives good results and is an adaptation of a cake I found in *The Chocolate Book*, written by Christine France.

75 g (2$^1/_2$ oz) dark chocolate, chopped

1 cup plain (all-purpose) flour

1 teaspoon baking powder

salt

110 g (3$^1/_2$ oz) unsalted butter, softened

110 g (3$^1/_2$ oz) crunchy peanut butter

1 cup brown sugar

2 large eggs, beaten

$^1/_4$ cup milk

Preheat the oven to 180°C (350°F, Gas Mark 4). Grease a 19 × 9 × 6.5 cm (7.5 × 3.5 × 2.5 in) loaf tin and line the base with baking paper.

Melt the chocolate in a heatproof bowl set over a saucepan of barely simmering water, stirring occasionally, until smooth. Allow to cool.

Sift together the flour, baking powder and a pinch of salt.

In an electric mixer, beat the butter, peanut butter and sugar for 3–4 minutes, or until pale and creamy. Gradually add the beaten eggs, alternating with spoonfuls of the flour, mixing well after each addition. Lightly fold in the remaining flour, alternating with the milk until just blended.

Pour half the mixture into a second bowl, add the chocolate and stir.

Using a large spoon, drop alternate spoonfuls of each mixture into the prepared tin. When all the mixture is in the tin, pull a large, flat knife through the batters to create a marbled effect. Bake for 45–55 minutes, or until golden and firm to the touch. A skewer inserted into the centre should come out clean. Turn out onto a wire rack to cool. Serve dusted with a little icing (confectioners') sugar.

christmas pudding.

My favourite Christmas pudding recipe comes from British food writer, Katie Stewart.

110 g (3¹/₂ oz) self-raising (self-rising) flour	2 large eggs
1 teaspoon mixed spice	juice and grated zest of 1 lemon
salt	1 tablespoon black treacle
75 g (2¹/₂ oz) fresh white breadcrumbs	175 g (6 oz) light muscovado sugar
30 g (1 oz) flaked almonds	110 g (3¹/₂ oz) butter
350 g (11 oz) mixed dried fruits	2 tablespoons brandy or rum, plus extra,
1 tart dessert apple, peeled, coarsely grated	to serve

Sift the flour, mixed spice and a pinch of salt into a large mixing bowl. Add the breadcrumbs, flaked almonds, dried fruit and apple.

In a jug, combine the eggs, lemon juice, zest and the treacle. Melt the muscovado sugar and butter in a saucepan over low heat. Pour the butter mixture and the egg mixture into the dry ingredients and mix. Cover with a cloth and allow to stand for 1 hour.

Mix again. Butter a 1.2-litre pudding basin. Spoon in the mixture, ensuring the top is level. Cover with buttered baking paper containing a few small pleats, then cover the top of the basin with pleated foil and secure with string.

To steam the pudding, preheat the oven to 150°C (300°F, Gas Mark 2). Place the pudding in a deep baking tin and pour boiling water into the baking tin to a depth of 2.5 cm (1 in). Cover the tin with a tent of foil and cook for 4–5 hours.

Let the pudding cool completely. Discard the coverings. Spoon over the brandy and re-cover. Store somewhere cool for up to 4 months – the refrigerator is a good place.

To serve the pudding, let it come to room temperature, re-cover with buttered baking paper and secure with foil, and steam for 2 hours. Invert the pudding onto a warm serving plate and remove the bowl. Flame the pudding with brandy, if desired.

Serves 8–10

cocoa.

¹/₂ cup Dutch cocoa

¹/₃ cup caster (superfine) sugar

3 cups milk

1 teaspoon vanilla essence

whipped cream and marshmallows
(optional), to serve

Sift the cocoa and sugar into a medium-sized saucepan. Add 1 cup of water and whisk over low heat for 2–3 minutes, or until the sugar has dissolved and the mixture is smooth. Add the milk, increase the heat to medium and cook for 10–12 minutes, whisking regularly, or until steam rises from the surface and tiny bubbles form around the edge. Do not let the mixture boil – taste it occasionally with a spoon to check the temperature. The regular whisking helps make the cocoa nice and frothy.

Stir in the vanilla. Pour the cocoa into four cups or mugs, top with whipped cream and marshmallows, if desired, and serve immediately.

The secret to cocoa with a deep chocolate flavour is to use both water and milk.

If you want to increase or decrease the quantity of the recipe above, the key ratio to remember is 1½ tablespoons of cocoa to 1 heaped tablespoon of sugar per cup of liquid.

Serves 4

corned beef (silverside).

1 × 1.5–2 kg (3–4 lb) piece corned beef
    (silverside)
4 onions, peeled and quartered
6 carrots, cut into 5 cm (2 in) pieces
2 bay leaves
handful of parsley stems
6–8 whole black peppercorns
¹/₂ star anise (optional, but good)

6 carrots, extra, sliced into 1 cm (¹/₂ in)
    pieces
12 small potatoes, scrubbed
1 small cabbage, halved, cored and cut into
    4 cm (1¹/₂ in) wedges
350 g (11 oz) fresh or frozen shelled peas
2 tablespoons chopped parsley
mustard-flavoured mayonnaise (see below)

Soak the corned beef in a very large saucepan of cold water for 3–4 hours (or overnight). Drain off the liquid and cover the meat with plenty of fresh cold water. Add the onion, carrot, bay leaves, parsley stems, peppercorns and star anise. Bring to the boil and simmer gently for 2½ hours.

Skim off the fat with a large spoon. Remove and discard the vegetables and ladle off half of the cooking liquid. Add the extra carrots and the potatoes and cabbage, and bring back to the boil. Cook for 20 minutes. Add the peas and cook for a further 5 minutes, or until the vegetables are tender.

Remove the beef and carve it into 1 cm (½ in) thick slices. Serve in large pasta bowls, surrounded by the vegetables. Ladle over a little cooking liquid and sprinkle with the parsley. Serve with a dollop of mustard-flavoured mayonnaise.

Make mustard mayonnaise by stirring 1 teaspoon of hot, ready-made mustard and 1 teaspoon of lemon juice into ½ cup of homemade or good-quality bought mayonnaise.

Serves 6

creamed corn.

Proper homemade creamed corn makes a great side dish to grilled steak or
barbecued sausages, and a delicious companion to roast chicken.
Corn is in season from summer to early autumn, so take advantage of this
sweet-tasting vegetable while it's available.

4 fresh cobs of corn
30 g (1 oz) butter
1 small onion, chopped

$^3/_4$ cup cream
salt and freshly ground black pepper

To prepare the corn, discard the husks and silk from the cobs. Rinse quickly and pat
dry. Stand a cob upright on a chopping board and, using a sharp knife, slice downwards,
cutting the kernels from the cob. Repeat with the remaining cobs.

Melt the butter in a medium-sized saucepan over gentle heat and add the onion.
Sauté for 4–5 minutes, or until tender. Add the corn kernels and cook over medium
heat, stirring occasionally, for 8 minutes. Stir in the cream, cover the pan, reduce the
heat a little and cook, stirring occasionally, for 10 minutes, or until the corn is tender
and the mixture is slightly thickened. Season well with salt and pepper.

The kernels should be nicely coated with cream – add a little extra if needed, or
reduce the sauce over high heat if there is too much liquid. Be careful not to let the
cream catch. Serve hot.

*Buy corn as fresh as possible and eat it soon after purchasing. When selecting corn to buy, look for
firm green cobs with clean white silks.*

*Creamed corn is also good with the addition of a little chopped red chilli and some freshly
snipped chives.*

Serves 4–6

crème brûlée.

2¹/₂ cups cream
1 vanilla bean or 1 teaspoon vanilla essence
8 egg yolks

¹/₄ cup caster (superfine) sugar
caster (superfine) sugar, extra, to serve

Preheat the oven to 180°C (350°F, Gas Mark 4).

Pour the cream into a medium-sized saucepan. Using a sharp knife, split the vanilla bean in half lengthways. Scrape out the seeds and add the pod and the seeds to the saucepan of cream. Bring the mixture to simmering point over low heat.

In a large mixing bowl, whisk together the egg yolks and sugar for 2 minutes. Gently whisk the hot milk mixture, including the vanilla bean, into the yolk mixture. Return this mixture to the saucepan and cook over low heat, stirring constantly with a wooden spoon, until the mixture thickens slightly to form a custard that coats the back of the spoon. Do not allow the mixture to boil or it will curdle. Remove from the heat and strain into a jug, discarding the vanilla pod. Divide the mixture between 6 × 7.5 cm (3 in) diameter ramekins, filling each almost to the top.

Transfer the ramekins to a large baking tin and fill the tin with enough boiling to water to come halfway up the sides of the ramekins. Carefully transfer to the oven and bake for 20–25 minutes, or until the custard has just set.

Remove ramekins from the water bath, allow to cool and chill overnight.

To finish the crème brûlées, cover the top of the custards with a thin, even layer of caster sugar. Place the ramekins on an oven tray and set them under a very hot grill, until the sugar has melted and coloured, adding a little more sugar if needed.

If using a grill to finish the brûlée, a good tip is to place the ramekins in a shallow dish and surround them with ice – this helps to stop the custard becoming soft under the heat.

Makes 6–8

crêpes with lemon and sugar.

125 g (4 oz) plain (all-purpose) flour
salt
1 large egg
1 large egg yolk
1 cup milk

30 g (1 oz) butter, melted
20 g ($^3/_4$ oz) butter, extra, for cooking
caster (superfine) sugar, to serve
lemon juice, to serve

Sift the flour and a pinch of salt into a mixing bowl. Add the egg, egg yolk and half of the milk. Using a wooden spoon, stir from the centre, gradually drawing in the flour from around the sides of the bowl. Gradually add the remaining milk and stir in ¼ cup of water and the melted butter. Beat well with the spoon until smooth.

Transfer the mixture to a jug and allow to stand for 30 minutes in a cool place. The batter will thicken on standing, so add a little more milk if needed before cooking – the batter should be the thickness of cream.

Heat an 18–20 cm (7–8 in) frying or crêpe pan over medium heat and, when hot, add a little butter. Pour approximately ¼ cup of batter into the pan and tilt the pan in a circular motion so that the batter evenly coats the surface. Cook for 2 minutes, or until the underside is light brown. Use a spatula to flip it and cook the other side. Remove to a warm plate.

Wipe the pan with a little extra butter and repeat the cooking process with the remaining batter. Layer the crêpes between slices of greaseproof paper to keep warm.

To serve, fold each crêpe in half, sprinkle with sugar and lemon juice and fold in half again. Serve extra sugar and wedges of lemon at the table.

Makes 8

curry powder.

Making your own freshly ground and blended curry powder will fill your kitchen
with exotic scents and your cupboard with a useful and delicious preparation.
There are many variations of this popular Indian curry mix; the following
blend is spicy, but not too hot. Homemade blends allow you to vary and
adjust the flavour and spice to your individual taste.

$^1/_4$ cup coriander seeds

1 tablespoon cumin seeds

1 tablespoon mustard seeds

1 teaspoon cardamom seeds, pods removed

8 whole cloves

1 × 5 cm (2 in) cinnamon stick, broken up

$^1/_2$ teaspoon freshly grated nutmeg

1–2 dried red chillies

2 tablespoons ground turmeric

Place the coriander, cumin, mustard and cardamom seeds, and the cloves and cinnamon, in a small frying pan. Place the pan over medium heat and toast the spices, stirring frequently, for 1–2 minutes. The spices will colour slightly and give off a wonderfully aromatic scent.

Allow to cool in the pan, then combine with the remaining ingredients. Grind to a fine powder in a mortar and pestle, spice mill or electric coffee grinder. Store in an airtight container in a cool, dark place for up to 6 months.

Increase the heat, if that's what you like, by adding more dried or powdered chillies.

An electric coffee grinder makes a great tool for grinding spices, but remember to use it just for spices.

custard.

75 ml (2$^1/_2$ fl oz) milk

2$^1/_2$ cups cream

1 vanilla bean

6 egg yolks

100 g (3$^1/_2$ oz) caster (superfine) sugar

1 heaped tablespoon cornflour (cornstarch)

Pour the milk and cream into a small saucepan. Using a sharp knife, split the vanilla bean in half lengthways. Scrape out the seeds and add the pod and the seeds to the saucepan. Bring the mixture to simmering point over low heat.

In a large mixing bowl, whisk together the egg yolks, sugar and cornflour for 2–3 minutes. Gently whisk the hot milk mixture, including the vanilla bean pod, into the yolk mixture. Return this mixture to the saucepan and cook over low heat, stirring constantly with a wooden spoon, until the mixture just reaches simmering point and is thick and smooth. Remove from the heat and strain through a coarse sieve into a bowl, discarding the vanilla bean pod.

Serve warm or at room temperature. If not using immediately, cover the surface with plastic wrap to prevent a skin forming.

Nothing beats the flavour of a fresh vanilla bean, but if you don't have one to hand use 1 teaspoon of pure vanilla essence.

Makes 3 cups

damper.

Damper is true Australian bush food – traditionally made by the campfire in the
outback and cooked in the coals of a fire. It's a quick and easy bread risen
with the use of baking powder rather than yeast.

3 cups self-raising (self-rising) flour
1 teaspoon baking powder
2 teaspoons caster (superfine) sugar
1 teaspoon salt

30 g (1 oz) butter, chilled and chopped
300 ml (9$^1/_2$ fl oz) milk, soured with
1 teaspoon lemon juice

Preheat the oven to 200°C (400°F, Gas Mark 6). Lightly grease an oven tray.

Sift the flour, baking powder, sugar and salt into a large mixing bowl. Rub the
butter into the flour mixture with your fingertips until it resembles breadcrumbs. Make
a well in the centre.

Mix together the milk and lemon juice – the mixture will curdle slightly – and pour
into the flour mixture. Mix gently, just until a soft dough forms. If the dough is too dry,
add milk, a tablespoon at a time, and mix.

Gather into a rough ball shape, turn out onto a lightly floured surface and knead
gently. The dough should feel slightly damp. With floured hands, pat the dough into
a round loaf shape and place it on the prepared oven tray. Sprinkle the loaf with a little
flour and slash a cross in the top with a sharp knife, if desired.

Bake for 25–30 minutes, or until risen and golden and the loaf sounds hollow
when tapped on the base. Remove from the tray and wrap in a clean cloth. Serve warm
or cold.

Makes 1 loaf

dumplings.

Dumplings are a great addition to a soup or a casserole. Prepare them about
30 minutes before you are ready to serve the dish, then, approximately
20 minutes before the end of cooking time, arrange the dumplings on
top of the soup or casserole, cover and continue cooking.

125 g (4 oz) self-raising (self-rising) flour	2 tablespoons chopped parsley
50 g (1³/₄ oz) shredded suet	salt and freshly ground black pepper

Sift the flour into a bowl and stir in the suet and parsley. Season with a little salt and
freshly ground black pepper. Add enough cold water (approximately 3–4 tablespoons)
to form a soft dough. Using lightly floured hands, pinch off walnut-sized pieces of
dough and roll them into small dumplings.

Arrange the dumplings on top of the soup or casserole, cover and cook for a further
20 minutes.

*Cheese and chive dumplings can be made by adding 30 g (1 oz) of grated cheddar or parmesan
to the basic recipe and replacing the parsley with 1 tablespoon of snipped fresh chives.*

Makes about 12

eggplant parmigiana.

4 medium-sized eggplants (aubergines)

salt

2 × 400 g (13 oz) cans chopped tomatoes

1 clove garlic, chopped

$^1/_4$ cup torn basil

salt, extra, and freshly ground black pepper

vegetable oil, for frying

2 × 200 g ($6^1/_2$ oz) mozzarella balls

100 g ($3^1/_2$ oz) parmesan, freshly grated

Cut the eggplants lengthways into slices about 1 cm (½ in) thick. Place in a large colander, sprinkle generously with salt and leave for at least 1 hour.

Rinse eggplant and dry well with kitchen paper.

Meanwhile, place the tomato, garlic and 1 tablespoon of the basil in a small saucepan and cook, stirring occasionally, over medium heat for about 15 minutes, or until thickened a little. Season well with salt and freshly ground black pepper.

Preheat the oven to 180°C (350°F, Gas Mark 4).

Cover the base of a large frying pan with vegetable oil. Place over medium–high heat and fry the eggplant slices in batches, until golden on both sides. Drain well on kitchen paper.

Cut the mozzarella balls into thin slices. Place a layer of eggplant in a 25 cm (10 in) square ovenproof dish and cover with a thin layer of the tomato sauce. Top with slices of mozzarella, a sprinkling of the parmesan and a little of the chopped basil. Lightly season with salt and pepper. Repeat these layers until the dish is full, finishing with tomato sauce and a sprinkling of parmesan.

Bake for 50–60 minutes, or until golden and bubbling. Leave to rest for 20 minutes before serving.

Salting eggplant helps to remove any bitter juices. It also retards oil absorption during cooking.

Serves 4

feta, cheddar and chive muffins.

2¹/₂ cups self-raising (self-rising) flour
¹/₂ teaspoon bicarbonate of soda
    (sodium bicarbonate)
salt
2 teaspoons snipped chives
75 g (2¹/₂ oz) feta, cut into ¹/₂ cm (¹/₄ in)
    cubes
50 g (1³/₄ oz) parmesan, grated
freshly ground black pepper
150 g (5 oz) cheddar, grated
300 ml (9¹/₂ fl oz) buttermilk
2 eggs, lightly beaten
100 g (3¹/₂ oz) butter, melted

Preheat the oven to 190°C (375°F, Gas Mark 5). Grease a 12-cup muffin tin or line with paper patty cases.

Sift the flour, bicarbonate of soda and a pinch of salt into a mixing bowl. Stir in the chives, feta, parmesan, a couple of grindings of black pepper and most of the cheddar – reserve a little to sprinkle on the top of the muffins. Make a well in the centre.

Whisk together the buttermilk, eggs and melted butter. Pour the egg mixture into the well in the flour mixture and stir until the ingredients are just combined. Do not over-mix – the batter should not be smooth.

Divide the mixture evenly between the muffin cups. Sprinkle with the remaining cheddar and bake for 25–30 minutes, or until the tops are firm to the touch and golden. Allow to cool in the tin for 5 minutes before turning out onto a wire rack.

If you don't have any buttermilk, use 1 teaspoon of lemon juice mixed with 300 ml (9½ fl oz) low-fat milk.

These muffins are best eaten on the day they are made and are delicious with a little butter.

Makes 12

fish lasagne.

750 g (1¹/₂ lb) smoked haddock or
    cod fillets
3 cups milk
3 eggs, at room temperature
1 tablespoon vegetable oil
4 rashers bacon
250 g (8 oz) uncooked tiger prawns
    (shrimp), shelled

75 g (2¹/₂ oz) butter
50 g (1³/₄ oz) plain (all-purpose) flour
150 ml (4¹/₂ oz) cream
175 g (6 oz) cheddar, roughly grated
salt and freshly ground black pepper
250 g (8 oz) fresh lasagne sheets
2 heaped tablespoons freshly grated
    parmesan

Preheat the oven to 190°C (375°F, Gas Mark 5). Place the fish in a baking tin, pour over the milk, cover with foil and bake for 25–30 minutes, or until just cooked.

Meanwhile, hardboil the eggs, peel, and roughly chop. Set aside in a large bowl.

Grill the bacon until cooked, then chop and add to the eggs, along with the prawns.

Remove the fish, reserving the milk. Flake the fish into bite-sized pieces, discarding the skin, and add it to the bacon and eggs.

Melt the butter in a medium-sized saucepan over low heat. Mix in the flour, cook for 1 minute, then slowly pour in the reserved milk, stirring constantly, then the cream. Stir until thickened. Add the cheddar, let it melt, then season lightly with salt and freshly ground black pepper. Remove from the heat and set aside.

Lightly grease a 20 × 20 × 6 cm (8 × 8 × 2½ in) ovenproof dish.

Layer the lasagne, starting with a third of the fish mixture. Cover with a thin layer of sauce and top with a layer of lasagne sheets. Repeat this process twice more, finishing with a final layer of sauce. Scatter with the parmesan.

Bake for 35 minutes, or until the lasagne is cooked. Cover with foil if the top becomes too brown during cooking.

Serves 6

focaccia.

1 × 7 g (¹/₄ oz) sachet (2 teaspoons) dry
    yeast
1 teaspoon sugar
2¹/₂ cups bread flour
salt

¹/₃ cup olive oil
2–3 tablespoons extra-virgin olive oil, plus
    extra to serve
sea salt, to sprinkle

Dissolve the yeast and sugar in a small bowl with 200 ml (6½ oz) of tepid water. Stir well and set aside for 10 minutes, or until the mixture froths.

Place the flour and a pinch of salt in a large mixing bowl. Make a well in the centre and add the yeast mixture and olive oil. Mix until a firm dough forms.

Knead on a lightly floured surface for 5–7 minutes, or until smooth and elastic. Place in a clean, lightly oiled bowl, cover with a cloth or plastic wrap and stand in a warm place for 1–1½ hours, or until the dough has doubled in size.

Punch down the dough with your fist to expel the air. Gently knead for 2 minutes and place on an oven tray. Using your fingertips, press the dough into a 30 × 18 cm (12 × 7 in) rectangle. Cover and leave in a warm spot to rise for 45 minutes.

Preheat the oven to 220°C (425°F, Gas Mark 7).

Press dimples into the surface of the dough. Brush well with the extra-virgin olive oil and sprinkle with sea salt. Bake for 20 minutes, spraying the oven with water from an atomiser at least three times during the first 10 minutes. Then slide the loaf off the tray onto the oven shelf and cook for a further 5 minutes, or until golden brown. Remove and serve drizzled with a little extra-virgin olive oil.

Make rosemary focaccia by brushing the dough with a combination of 2 tablespoons of roughly chopped rosemary and the extra-virgin olive oil before baking.

free-form blueberry pie.

1 quantity homemade regular shortcrust
    pastry (see page 106), or 1 × 380 g
    (12 oz) packet bought frozen
    shortcrust pastry, thawed
100 g (3¹/₂ oz) crushed amaretti biscuits or
    cake crumbs

500 g (1 lb) fresh blueberries
¹/₃ cup caster (superfine) sugar
1 egg, beaten
sugar, to sprinkle

Prepare the pastry according to the instructions on page 106 and refrigerate for at least 30 minutes.

Preheat the oven to 200°C (400°F, Gas Mark 6).

On a lightly floured surface, roll out the pastry to make a 35 cm (14 in) circle. Sprinkle the pastry with the biscuit crumbs, leaving a 5 cm (2 in) border. Pile on the blueberries, keeping them within the border, and sprinkle with the caster sugar. Fold up the edges of the pastry to form a freeform-shaped pie (see picture). Brush the pastry with the beaten egg and sprinkle the pastry with sugar, to decorate.

Bake for 25–30 minutes, or until the pastry is golden and the berries have softened. Serve warm or cold.

This pie is good with vanilla ice-cream.

If making your own pastry, add 1 tablespoon of caster (superfine) sugar to the flour mixture as a variation.

Serves 6–8

fresh vietnamese spring rolls.

30 g (1 oz) rice vermicelli (cellophane)
    noodles
24 medium-sized cooked prawns (shrimp),
    shelled and roughly chopped
juice of 1 lime
$^1/_2$ teaspoon Thai fish sauce
$^1/_2$ Lebanese cucumber, peeled and thinly
    sliced

1 carrot, peeled and very thinly sliced
1 cup pea shoots
$^1/_2$ cup mint leaves
$^1/_2$ cup coriander (cilantro) leaves
salt and freshly ground black pepper
12 × 15 cm (6 in) square Asian rice paper
    wrappers
dipping sauce (see below)

Place the noodles in a heatproof bowl and cover with boiling water. Leave to soak for 5 minutes, or until tender. Drain well, blot with kitchen paper and cut into 5 cm (2 in) strips with scissors.

Combine the noodles, prawns, lime juice, fish sauce, cucumber, carrot, pea shoots, mint and coriander in a bowl. Season with salt and pepper.

Fill a shallow bowl with hot water. Dip six rice paper wrappers in the water for a minute to soften. Remove and place in a single layer on a clean tea towel.

Divide half the noodle mixture between the wrappers, spreading the mixture down the centre of each wrapper in a log shape. Fold up the base of each wrapper and then tightly roll sideways. Transfer to a serving plate and cover with a damp cloth. Repeat with the remaining rice paper wrappers and mixture. Serve with the dipping sauce.

To make the dipping sauce, stir together 2 teaspoons of brown sugar, 2 tablespoons of fresh lime juice, 2 teaspoons of Thai fish sauce and 1 chopped small red chilli. Serve in a small bowl.

Makes 12

fruit tart.

1 quantity homemade regular shortcrust
pastry (see page 106), or 1 × 380 g
(12 oz) packet bought frozen shortcrust
pastry, thawed
300 ml (9¹/₂ fl oz) cream
¹/₂ cup plain natural yoghurt

¹/₂ cup lightly packed brown sugar
500 g (1 lb) ripe strawberries, hulled and
halved
2 tablespoons icing (confectioners') sugar
juice of ¹/₂ orange
1 teaspoon balsamic vinegar

Prepare the pastry according to the instructions on page 106.

Lightly grease a 21 cm (8½ in) loose-based fluted tart tin. Roll out the pastry between two sheets of baking paper until it is large enough to fit the tart tin. Line the tin with the pastry and trim the edges. Refrigerate for 15 minutes.

Preheat the oven to 200°C (400°F, Gas Mark 6).

Line the pastry case with baking paper. Half-fill the pastry case with pie weights, uncooked dried beans or rice. Bake for 10–15 minutes. Remove the weights and baking paper, return the tin to the oven and cook for a further 10 minutes, or until the pastry is dry and golden. Set aside to cool.

Whip the cream until soft peaks form, then stir in the yoghurt. Spoon the mixture into the tart shell – it should be about three-quarters full. Sprinkle the cream mixture with an even layer of brown sugar. Set aside for 30 minutes.

Meanwhile, place the strawberries in a bowl, sprinkle with the icing sugar and drizzle with the orange juice and balsamic vinegar.

Just before serving, fill the tart with a layer of strawberries.

You can replace the strawberries with any ripe summer fruit. Try a combination of peaches and raspberries, or mango and passionfruit.

Serves 8

gravlax.

This Swedish dish preserves fresh salmon by marinating it in a mixture of salt and sugar. The preparation time is minimal and the curing process occurs in the refrigerator.

2 tablespoons roughly chopped fresh dill

150 g (5 oz) sea salt

100 g (3^1/$_2$ oz) sugar

2 tablespoons freshly ground black pepper

1 tablespoon vodka or vermouth

2 large salmon fillets – total weight about 1.25 kg (2 lb 7 oz)

In a bowl, combine the dill, salt, sugar, pepper and vodka. Spread a quarter of the mixture on the base of a ceramic dish that is big enough to hold the salmon fillets.

Place one fillet, skin-side down, on top of the mixture. Cover with slightly more than half of the remaining salt mixture. Place the second fillet on top, skin-side up, and scatter the remaining salt mixture over the skin. Seal the dish with plastic wrap, then weigh down the salmon with tins or a heavy breadboard. Refrigerate for at least 24 hours (maximum 48 hours), turning the fish every 12 hours.

When ready to serve, drain off any liquid, brush off the marinade and wipe dry with kitchen paper. Slice the salmon thinly – it will look slightly translucent. Serve as you would smoked salmon.

Gravlax is traditionally served with rye bread and a mustard dressing. Make the dressing by combining 1 tablespoon of Dijon mustard, 1 teaspoon of caster (superfine) sugar and 2 tablespoons of wine vinegar. Gradually whisk in ½ cup of vegetable oil until amalgamated. Stir in 1 tablespoon of chopped dill and season to taste with salt and freshly ground black pepper.

Once cured, the salmon will keep in the refrigerator for up to 5 days.

greek salad.

As per the authentic Athenian way, this version of a Greek salad serves everything nice and chunky, without any lettuce. This delicious recipe is from Terry Durack.

3 ripe tomatoes

1 crisp cucumber, unpeeled

2 tablespoons Greek olive oil

1 tablespoon lemon juice or red-wine
    vinegar

sea salt and freshly ground black pepper

200 g ($6^1/_2$ oz) Greek feta, in one piece

20 Kalamata olives

$^1/_2$ red (Spanish) onion, sliced into thin
    rings

1 teaspoon chopped fresh oregano or dill

$^1/_2$ teaspoon dried oregano

Cut the tomatoes into quarters or eighths. Cut the cucumber in half lengthwise, and roughly chop. Toss the tomato and cucumber with the olive oil and lemon juice, and season to taste with salt and freshly ground black pepper. Top with the feta in one piece and scatter with the olives, onion rings and herbs. Break up the feta with a fork as you serve.

This recipe serves two people as a light lunch. The quantities can easily be doubled if needed.

Serves 2

green fish curry.

This is a simple variation of a Thai green curry. The coconut milk adds smoothness and balances the spices and the heat.

1 tablespoon vegetable oil

1 shallot or small onion, thinly sliced

1 teaspoon grated fresh ginger

3–4 tablespoons homemade Thai green curry paste (see page 164), or good-quality bought Thai green curry paste

2 cups coconut milk

1 teaspoon palm or brown sugar

1 kg (2 lb) blue-eye cod fillets or other large white fish fillets, cut into 5 cm (2 in) pieces

1 tablespoon Thai fish sauce

juice of 1 lime

1 cup lightly packed coriander (cilantro) or basil leaves, to serve

salt

1 lime, to serve

Heat the oil in a large saucepan and add the shallot and ginger. Cook over medium heat, stirring occasionally, for 3 minutes. Add the curry paste and cook, stirring, for a further minute.

Add the coconut milk and sugar and bring to the boil. Reduce the heat and simmer gently, stirring occasionally, for 15 minutes – this allows the flavours to develop.

Add the fish pieces, stir well and cook for 5 minutes, or until tender. Use a spoon to remove any oil that rises to the top. Stir in the fish sauce, lime juice and half the coriander. Season to taste with salt. Serve with steamed rice and a lime quarter, and garnish with the remaining coriander.

Vary the amount of curry paste to suit your taste.

Serves 4

grilled peaches.

A sweet, sun-ripened peach is a real summer treat. Take advantage of this delicious fruit by creating this simple and tasty dessert. Grilling peaches seems to bring out their natural flavour. Serving them with fresh raspberries is a perfect match.

4 ripe slipstone peaches	**cream or ice-cream, to serve**
$^1/_3$ cup sugar	**raspberries, to serve**

Preheat the grill to hot.

Peel the peaches, if desired, then cut in half and remove the stones.

Place the peach halves cut-side up in a baking tin. Sprinkle with the sugar and grill for 5–8 minutes, or until the sugar has caramelised and the fruit has begun to brown. Transfer to four serving plates and serve immediately with dollops of thick cream or with scoops of good-quality vanilla ice-cream and fresh raspberries.

Choose large, ripe peaches that smell fragrant and are slightly soft when pressed.

Grilled peaches are also delicious sprinkled with a little Cointreau or amaretto before cooking.

Dollops of mascarpone or vanilla yoghurt also go particularly well with this dessert.

Nectarines make a good substitute for peaches.

Serves 4

hamburgers.

250 g (8 oz) minced (ground) beef

2 tablespoons tomato sauce (ketchup)

dash of Worcestershire sauce

salt and freshly ground black pepper

1 tablespoon vegetable oil

butter

2 good-quality bread rolls, split in half

50 g (2 oz) rocket (arugula) leaves

1 ripe tomato, sliced

1 cooked beetroot, sliced

Combine the meat, tomato sauce and Worcestershire sauce. Season with plenty of salt and freshly ground black pepper. Divide the mixture in two and shape each portion into a 10 cm (4 in) diameter patty. Do not over-handle the meat – it will toughen the hamburgers.

Heat the oil in a heavy frying pan over medium–high heat. When the oil is hot, add the burgers and cook for 1–2 minutes, or until browned. Turn and cook for a further minute, or until well browned.

Meanwhile, lightly butter the rolls and cover the bottom half of each with a layer of rocket leaves. Top each with a burger and then a layer of tomato and beetroot. Season lightly and top with the other half of the roll.

Don't use low-fat minced meat for burgers, as a little bit of fat will make the burgers juicier. I often add 2 finely chopped rashers of bacon to the burger mixture.

Don't forget to offer tomato sauce, barbecue sauce or mayonnaise with the burgers.

Makes 2

hazelnut slice.

120 g (4 oz) skinned hazelnuts

50 g (1$^3/_4$ oz) dark chocolate, chopped

60 g (2 oz) butter, chopped

1 teaspoon instant coffee powder

1 cup caster (superfine) sugar

$^1/_2$ cup plain (all-purpose) flour

$^1/_2$ teaspoon baking powder

2 eggs, lightly beaten

1 teaspoon vanilla essence

icing (confectioners') sugar, to serve

Preheat the oven to 180°C (350°F, Gas Mark 4). Lightly grease a shallow 20 cm (8 in) square cake tin and line the base and sides with baking paper, leaving the paper overhanging on two opposite sides.

Place the hazelnuts in a baking tin and roast in the oven for 5 minutes, tossing occasionally, or until lightly toasted. Cool and roughly chop.

Melt the chocolate and butter with the coffee powder in a heatproof bowl set over a saucepan of barely simmering water, stirring occasionally, until melted and smooth. Remove from the heat.

Sift the sugar, flour and baking powder into the chocolate and butter mixture. Add the eggs, vanilla and half of the hazelnuts. Mix with a wooden spoon until combined.

Spoon the mixture into the prepared cake tin and bake for 15 minutes. Remove, top with the remaining hazelnuts and return to the oven for a further 20 minutes, or until firm and nicely coloured. Leave to cool in the tin for 10 minutes before removing the slice using the overhanging baking paper. Allow to cool on a wire rack. To serve, dust with icing (confectioners') sugar and cut into squares.

Makes 16

honeycomb.

A candy thermometer is a useful piece of kitchen equipment and a good investment.
Using a candy thermometer enables you to know when the correct temperature
is reached – very important when making candies, fudge or jam.

2 cups sugar

¹/₄ cup golden syrup

1 teaspoon bicarbonate of soda

(sodium bicarbonate)

Lightly grease a 20 × 30 cm (8 × 12 in) shallow cake tin.

Combine the sugar, golden syrup and 1 cup of water in a medium-sized saucepan. Place over medium heat and bring to the boil, stirring to dissolve the sugar. Gently boil the mixture, without stirring, for 5–10 minutes, or until it reaches 154°C (310°F) or hard-crack stage on the thermometer. Remove the pan from the heat and sprinkle the bicarbonate of soda over the mixture. It will immediately froth and foam up. Beat quickly with a balloon whisk for about 5 seconds, then pour the mixture into the prepared tin.

Allow to cool for a few minutes before scoring into bars or squares. When completely cool, turn out of the tin onto a breadboard and cut into pieces.

Honeycomb is delicious broken into bite-sized pieces and dipped in melted chocolate.

Make hokey-pokey ice-cream by stirring crushed pieces of honeycomb into softened vanilla icecream. Refreeze before serving.

kedgeree.

Kedgeree is a dish the British brought home from their days in India – the rice and spices are typically Indian, and the smoked fish and eggs are the result of Anglo adaptation. The recipe I always use is by Katie Stewart.

900 g (1 lb 13 oz) smoked fish (haddock or cod) fillets
1 bay leaf
a few parsley stalks
1 tablespoon vegetable oil
100 g (3^1/$_2$ oz) butter
1 onion

^{1}/$_2$ teaspoon curry powder (see page 46)
450 g (14 oz) basmati or long-grained rice
3 large hard-boiled eggs
125 g (4 oz) unsalted cashews
^{1}/$_3$ cup chopped parsley
juice of ^{1}/$_2$ lemon
lemon or lime wedges, to serve

Cut the fish fillets into pieces about 5 cm (2 in) square, discarding any skin or bones. Place in a large saucepan with the bay leaf and parsley stalks, and cover with 1 litre (32 fl oz) of water. Bring to a simmer and poach the fish for 6 minutes, or until tender. Remove the fish pieces with a slotted spoon. Strain the cooking liquid and reserve. When the fish is cool, break the flesh into loose flakes.

Heat the oil and half of the butter in a saucepan over low heat. Add the onion and cook gently for 5 minutes, or until softened. Add the curry powder and rice and stir into the butter and onion for a moment. Add the reserved poaching liquid. Bring to a simmer, stirring occasionally, then cover and cook over gentle heat for 20–25 minutes, or until the rice is tender and all the liquid has been absorbed.

Shell and chop the hard-boiled eggs. Using a fork, fold the eggs, fish, cashews, parsley, lemon juice and remaining butter into the cooked rice. Heat gently until hot, then serve at once with lemon wedges.

Serves 6–8

laksa.

I usually cheat a little and use a ready-made laksa paste to make this dish.

1 tablespoon vegetable oil

3–4 tablespoons laksa paste

600 ml (19 fl oz) coconut milk

600 ml (19 fl oz) fish or chicken stock

4 fresh kaffir lime leaves, thinly sliced
(optional)

200 g (6¹/₂ oz) rice vermicelli (cellophane)
noodles

24 medium-sized uncooked prawns
(shrimp), shelled and deveined, or
2–3 cooked skinned chicken breasts,
chopped

100 g (3¹/₂ oz) bean sprouts

1 cup coriander (cilantro) leaves

8 bean curd puffs, each cut into 3 pieces

Thai fish sauce, to serve

2–3 teaspoons sambal oelek

1 lime, quartered

Heat the oil in a large frying pan over medium heat. Add the laksa paste and cook, stirring, for 2–3 minutes, or until fragrant. Add the coconut milk and stock and bring to the boil. Stir in the lime leaves. Reduce the heat and simmer for 10 minutes.

Meanwhile, place the noodles in a heatproof bowl and cover with boiling water. Leave to soak for 5 minutes, or until tender. Drain.

Add the prawns to the simmering broth and cook for 2 minutes, or until cooked.

Divide the noodles between four deep bowls. Add the prawns or chicken to the bowls and ladle the broth over the noodles. Garnish with the bean sprouts, coriander leaves and bean curd puffs. Drizzle each bowl with a little fish sauce and top with sambal oelek. Serve with lime quarters.

Serves 4

lamb shanks.

8 lamb shanks

$^1/_3$ cup plain (all-purpose) flour

$^1/_4$ cup vegetable oil

4 cloves garlic, crushed

2 onions, sliced

3 sticks celery, sliced

2 × 400 g (13 oz) cans chopped tomatoes

2 cups white wine

2 cups chicken or beef stock

2 large red chillies

2 sprigs rosemary

salt and freshly ground black pepper

GREMOLATA

1 clove garlic, finely chopped

$^1/_4$ cup finely chopped flat-leaf parsley

grated zest of 1 lemon

Preheat the oven to 160°C (315°F, Gas Mark 2–3). Coat the shanks with the flour.

Heat half the oil in a large frying pan over medium heat. Cook the shanks two or three at a time, adding a little extra oil if needed, until browned. Do not overcrowd the pan – the meat will start to stew. Transfer to a large casserole dish.

Heat the remaining oil in the frying pan over medium heat. Add the garlic, onion and celery and cook, stirring occasionally, for 6–7 minutes, or until the vegetables are tender but not coloured. Transfer to the casserole dish.

Stir the tomato, wine and stock into the casserole and bring to the boil over medium heat. Tuck the whole chillies and rosemary into the pot. Cover, transfer to the oven and cook for 2 hours. Turn the shanks occasionally as they cook.

Remove from the oven and check the sauce for seasoning.

To make the gremolata, combine the garlic, parsley and lemon zest. Serve up the shanks in their sauce, sprinkled with the gremolata.

Serves 4

lemon bars.

BASE
125 g (4 oz) unsalted butter, softened
1 cup caster (superfine) sugar
1¹/₃ cups plain (all-purpose) flour

LEMON TOPPING
1 cup caster (superfine) sugar

4 eggs
1 teaspoon grated lemon zest
¹/₂ cup freshly squeezed lemon juice
¹/₃ cup plain (all-purpose) flour
¹/₂ teaspoon baking powder
icing (confectioners') sugar, to serve

Lightly grease a 20 × 30 cm (8 × 12 in) shallow cake tin and line the base and sides with baking paper, leaving the paper overhanging along the two long sides.

Make the base by beating the butter and sugar together in a bowl for 3–4 minutes, or until pale and fluffy. Sift in the flour and fold through with a large metal spoon until combined and the mixture forms a firm dough. Press the mixture into the prepared tin, making sure there are no holes, and chill for 15 minutes.

Preheat the oven to 180°C (350°F , Gas Mark 4).

Bake the base for 20 minutes, or until firm and golden. Allow to cool in the tin.

Make the lemon topping by placing the sugar, eggs and lemon zest in a mixing bowl and beating with a hand-held electric mixer for 2–3 minutes, or until thickened and increased in volume. Stir in the lemon juice. Sift over the flour and baking powder and use the mixer on low spread to gradually whisk in.

Spoon the mixture onto the cool base, return to the oven and bake for 25–30 minutes, or until the topping is just set. Remove and allow to cool in the tin. Lift out using the baking paper and cut into 5 cm (2 in) squares. Serve dusted with icing (confectioners') sugar.

Makes 24

lemon chicken.

2 chicken breasts

2 chicken thighs with drumsticks attached

salt and freshly ground black pepper

2 lemons

2 cloves garlic, unpeeled

2 tablespoons olive oil

2 cups chicken stock or water
(approximately)

2 tablespoons roughly chopped
flat-leaf parsley

Preheat the oven to 200°C (400°F, Gas Mark 6).

Place the chicken pieces in a baking tin. Season well with salt and freshly ground black pepper. Quarter one of the lemons and squeeze the juice from two of the quarters over the chicken pieces. Add the four lemon quarters (including the squeezed ones) to the tin. Add the garlic cloves and drizzle the chicken with the oil. Roast for 30–35 minutes, or until tender and golden.

Remove the chicken and keep warm. Pour or spoon off any fat from the baking tin, and discard the lemon quarters. Add the juice from the remaining lemon to the tin, along with enough chicken stock to cover the bottom of the tin. Place over medium heat on the stove top, bring to the boil and stir well with a wooden spoon to loosen any bits stuck to the bottom of the tin. Squash the garlic with the back of the spoon to release any juices. Simmer gently for 5 minutes to reduce slightly, and season to taste with salt and freshly ground black pepper.

Pour the sauce over the chicken and sprinkle with the parsley. Serve immediately with a salad or steamed vegetables.

Serves 4

lemon ice-cream.

This rich ice-cream can be easily made without an ice-cream churn.

grated zest of 2 lemons

juice of 3 lemons

$^3/_4$ cup icing (confectioners') sugar

$1^1/_2$ cups cream

$^1/_2$ cup plain natural yoghurt

Mix the lemon zest, juice and icing sugar in a small bowl until combined.

In a separate, clean bowl, whip the cream until it holds soft peaks, then stir through the yoghurt.

Gently whisk the lemon juice mixture into the cream mixture, until smooth and combined. Pour into a shallow, lidded container, cover with a layer of baking paper and the lid, then place in the freezer for 4 hours, or until firm and frozen. Freeze, covered, for up to 2 weeks.

Prior to serving, soften the ice-cream by transferring it to the refrigerator for about 15 minutes.

The yoghurt gives this ice-cream a nice depth of flavour. Alternatively, you can make it with more cream instead of the yoghurt, if desired.

Serves 6

lemon posset.

This simple pudding is well pedigreed and was very popular in the 19th century, when sweet creams and syllabubs were much favoured. This dish is definitely worth reviving, as it magically sets to a form a sweet lemon custard using only cream, sugar and lemon juice. It is particularly delicious served with ripe berries.

600 ml (19 fl oz) double or thick cream
3/4 cup caster (superfine) sugar

juice of 2 lemons

Place the cream and sugar in a saucepan and slowly bring to the boil over low heat, stirring to dissolve the sugar. Boil gently for 3 minutes.

Remove from the heat and whisk in the lemon juice. Allow to cool slightly and pour into 4 × 200 ml (6½ fl oz) ramekins, small tea cups or glasses. Chill for 12 hours or until set.

Serves 4

macaroni cheese.

A big thanks to Nigel Slater for letting me include his 'really good macaroni cheese' recipe – a jolly nice supper dish.

350 g (11 oz) small macaroni, penne or
    other short, hollow dried pasta
1 litre (32 fl oz) milk
1 bay leaf
60 g (2 oz) butter
3 tablespoons plain (all-purpose) flour

6 rashers smoked streaky bacon
$^3/_4$ cup grated mature farmhouse cheddar
2 teaspoons Dijon mustard
salt and freshly ground black pepper
2 handfuls fresh breadcrumbs
$^1/_3$ cup freshly grated parmesan

Preheat the oven to 200°C (400°F, Gas Mark 6).

Cook the pasta in plenty of boiling salted water until it is al dente.

Meanwhile, warm the milk in a saucepan over medium heat and add the bay leaf. When the milk comes to the boil, remove it from the heat.

In another saucepan, melt the butter. Add the flour and stir over moderate heat until you have a pale, biscuit-coloured paste. Pour in the hot milk, discarding the bay leaf, and whisk until there are no lumps. Simmer until the sauce is the consistency of double cream, stirring regularly so it does not catch.

Grill the bacon until lightly crisp, then break it into small pieces. Drain the pasta and fold it into the sauce, along with the bacon, cheddar cheese and mustard, and season to taste with salt and freshly ground black pepper.

Tip the mixture into a 2-litre (64-fl oz) gratin dish, avoiding the temptation to smooth the top. Toss the breadcrumbs with the parmesan and scatter over the top. Bake for 35–40 minutes or until topping is golden.

Serves 4

madeleines.

2 eggs

60 g (2 oz) caster (superfine) sugar

1 teaspoon vanilla essence

$^1/_3$ cup plain (all-purpose) flour

50 g ($1^3/_4$ oz) butter, melted

icing (confectioners') sugar, to sprinkle

Preheat the oven to 180°C (350°F, Gas Mark 4). Generously grease and flour a 12-hole madeleine tin.

Whisk together the eggs and sugar for 2–3 minutes, or until the sugar has dissolved and the mixture is thick and pale and has increased in volume. Sift the flour on top and fold in gently with a large metal spoon. Gently stir in the melted butter until combined.

Fill each hole in the prepared tin to three-quarters full. Bake for 7–10 minutes, or until risen, golden and firm to the touch. Cool on a wire rack. Sprinkle lightly with icing sugar while still warm. Eat within a couple of hours of baking.

Madeleines are traditionally made in a tin with shallow, shell-shaped holes. Alternatively, you can use a shallow 12-cup muffin tin.

Madeleines are even more delicious with 1 teaspoon of grated orange or lemon zest added to the mixture.

Makes 12

maître d'hôtel butter.

Mâitre d'hôtel butter is traditionally served with steak, but it is also good with grilled fish. Top a grilled steak or fish fillet with a slice of butter.

100 g (3^1/$_2$ oz) unsalted butter, diced and
softened
2 tablespoons finely chopped parsley
1 teaspoon chopped chervil (optional)

^{1}/$_2$ teaspoon salt
freshly ground black pepper
1 tablespoon lemon juice

Place the butter, parsley, chervil and salt and a good grinding of freshly ground black pepper into a small bowl. Using a fork or wooden spoon, beat the mixture until the ingredients are combined. Slowly add the lemon juice, beating as you go, until combined.

Roll the butter into a small log. Wrap in baking paper and chill until firm. Store, wrapped in baking paper, in the refrigerator for up to 2 weeks. To serve, cut the butter into 1 cm (½ in) slices.

mango sorbet.

Easy to make, ultra refreshing and full of flavour, this sorbet is virtually fat free.
It can easily be made without an ice-cream churn. Mango sorbet is perfect served
simply in a cone or bowl.

170 g (5^1/$_2$ oz) caster (superfine) sugar	**2 large ripe mangoes, flesh removed and**
juice of 1 lime	**chopped**

Place the sugar in a heatproof bowl and pour over 1 cup of boiling water. Stir well until dissolved, then set aside to cool.

Purée the lime juice, mango and sugar syrup in a blender until smooth. Taste and add extra lime juice or sugar if desired. Churn in an ice-cream machine until firm. If you don't have a machine, pour the mixture into a shallow, lidded container and place, covered, in the freezer for about 2 hours, or until firm on top and frozen around the edges. Transfer to an electric mixer or food processor and beat or whiz until smooth. Return to the freezer until firm, then beat and freeze once more.

Freeze, covered, for up to 2 weeks. Prior to serving, soften the sorbet by transferring it to the refrigerator for about 15 minutes.

Variations to this recipe are numerous. Try one or all of the following: raspberry sorbet — replace the mango flesh with 500 g (1 lb) of raspberries (frozen raspberries are fine); strawberry sorbet — replace the mango flesh with 400 g (13 oz) of hulled strawberries; peach or nectarine sorbet — replace the mango flesh with 5 large ripe peaches or nectarines, peeled and roughly chopped.

Serves 4

marmalade.

1 kg (2 lb) Seville oranges
juice of 1 large lemon

2 kg (4 lb) sugar

Scrub the oranges to remove any wax on the peel. Place the whole oranges in a large saucepan with 2 litres of water. Bring to the boil, then simmer gently for 2 hours, or until the skin of the oranges is very soft and can be easily pierced with a fork.

Remove the fruit from the saucepan, reserving the cooking liquid. When cool enough to handle, quarter each orange and cut each segment into thin shreds, saving the juice. Remove any pips and place them on a 20 cm (8 in) square of muslin or cheese cloth. Tie the bag tightly with a piece of string – the string should be long enough to secure the bag and to allow it to be tied to the handle of the saucepan but reach the bottom of the pan.

Place a saucer in the freezer.

Return the cooking liquid to medium heat, add the pips and lemon juice and boil for 10 minutes. Remove the pips, then add the chopped fruit and reserved juice and boil until reduced by one third.

Add the sugar, stirring well to dissolve. Increase the heat and boil rapidly for about 20 minutes, or until setting point is reached. To test for setting point, drop a spoonful of marmalade onto the chilled saucer and allow to cool. If the jam forms a skin and wrinkles when pushed with a fingertip, it has reached setting point. Remove marmalade from heat when testing.

Allow the jam to cool, stir well, then spoon into sterilised jars, seal and label.

Makes 2½ litres

meat loaf.

This dish is inspired by a recipe that originally came from Delia Smith.

500 g (1 lb) minced (ground) veal

500 g (1 lb) minced (ground) pork

4 rashers streaky bacon, chopped

2 onions, finely chopped

2 cloves garlic, chopped

2 tablespoons chopped parsley

2 teaspoons chopped thyme

1 egg, lightly beaten

1 cup fresh white breadcrumbs

$^1/_4$ cup milk

2 teaspoons Dijon mustard

2 teaspoons Worcestershire sauce

$^1/_2$ cup beef stock or vegetable stock

salt and freshly ground black pepper

3 hard-boiled eggs, shells removed

Preheat the oven to 160°C (315°F, Gas Mark 2–3). Grease a 20 × 12 × 9 cm (9 × 5 × 3½ in) loaf tin.

In a large bowl, combine the veal, pork, bacon, onion, garlic, herbs and egg. Mix well with your hands or with a large wooden spoon.

In a separate bowl, lightly mash together the breadcrumbs and the milk, then add to the meat mixture. Stir in the mustard, Worcestershire sauce and stock. Season well.

Half fill the prepared tin with the mixture. Place the hard-boiled eggs end to end down the centre of the tin, then cover with the remaining mixture. Level the top and cover the tin with foil. Place in a large baking tin and fill the baking tin with enough boiling water to come one-third of the way up the sides of the loaf tin. Carefully transfer to the oven and bake for 2 hours, or until cooked. A skewer inserted into the centre and pressed should produce clear liquid, not pink liquid. Allow to cool in the tin for 15 minutes before serving. Serve hot or cold.

Meatloaf is delicious served hot with a spicy fresh tomato sauce or cold with pickles or chutney.

Serves 8

meringues.

3 large egg whites **salt**	**175 g (6 oz) caster (superfine) sugar**

Preheat the oven to 140°C (275°F, Gas Mark 1). Line two oven trays with baking paper.

Place the egg whites and a pinch of salt in a large, clean, dry bowl. Whisk with an electric mixer or hand-held electric beater on low speed for a couple of minutes. Increase the speed to medium and whisk for a further 2 minutes, or until stiff peaks form – if you lift the beater out of the bowl, the mixture should cling to the beaters, keeping stiff and moist-looking peaks. Continue to whisk the mixture, gradually adding the sugar 1 tablespoon at a time and beating well after each addition. Continue beating until the mixture is stiff and glossy – this may take 5–10 minutes.

Using a large metal spoon, spoon free-form shapes (2 rounded tablespoons in size) onto the prepared trays.

Bake the meringues for 15–20 minutes, or until pale and dry. Turn off the oven and allow to cool in the oven with the door ajar. Store in an airtight container for up to 2 weeks.

Instead of spooning the mixture onto the oven trays, alternatively you can use a piping bag. The easiest way to do this is to sit the bag in a large, tall glass or container and fold the top of the bag over the edge of the glass. Spoon in the mixture and secure the top of the bag with a few twists. Keeping the bag upright, pipe small shapes onto the tray.

Makes 40

mocha.

Chocolate and coffee are flavours made for each other. Just as the depth and flavour of a chocolate cake is improved with the addition of a little coffee, this hot chocolate drink is delicious when combined with coffee. This is a perfect lazy Sunday afternoon treat.

100 g (3^1/$_2$ oz) dark chocolate, chopped

2 teaspoons sugar

1 cup milk

a plunger or pot of freshly brewed coffee

whipped cream, to serve

cocoa, drinking chocolate or grated chocolate, to serve

Combine the chocolate, sugar and milk in a small saucepan. Place over low heat and stir until the sugar and chocolate have melted and the mixture is smooth. As it comes to the boil, whisk hard to create a bit of froth, then remove from the heat.

Divide the mixture between two large mugs and add enough freshly brewed coffee to almost fill the mugs. Top with a dollop of whipped cream and sprinkle with a little cocoa or grated chocolate. Taste and add extra sugar if desired.

Use good-quality couverture chocolate or dark chocolate with a high cocoa butter content, if available.

Mocha is also good with a dash of brandy, whisky or a flavoured liqueur, such as Frangelico or Grand Marnier.

Serves 2

mussel broth.

6 large ripe Roma (egg) tomatoes

2 tablespoons olive oil

2 leeks, thinly sliced

1 clove garlic, crushed

2 sticks celery, thinly sliced

1 large red chilli, seeded and sliced

1 cup white wine

1 cup vegetable stock or fish stock

2 kg (4 lb) fresh mussels, cleaned and debearded

$^1/_4$ cup roughly chopped flat-leaf parsley

salt and freshly ground black pepper

Cut a cross in the base of each tomato, then place tomatoes in a large heatproof bowl and pour over enough hot water to cover. Let them sit for 1 minute, then drain off the water. Peel the tomatoes by pulling the skin away from the end with the cross. Chop the peeled tomatoes and place them and any juice in a bowl.

Heat the oil in a large saucepan and add the leek, garlic, celery and chilli. Cook over medium heat, stirring occasionally, for 5 minutes, or until the vegetables have softened. Add the wine, stock and tomato (with the juice) and simmer over gentle heat for 5 minutes.

Add the mussels and increase the heat to high. Cover with a tight-fitting lid and cook for 3–4 minutes, giving the saucepan an occasional shake to help the mussels release their juices. Uncover, add the parsley and stir well. Season to taste with salt and freshly ground black pepper. Serve the mussels and broth in large, wide bowls with plenty of crusty bread.

When buying mussels, choose only those that have perfect shells. Prior to cooking, use only those that close firmly after giving them a good tap. If they haven't already been cleaned, soak mussels in fresh water for 15 minutes, then scrub them and pull off their beards with a sharp tug. Discard any mussels that don't open after cooking.

Serves 4

onion marmalade.

This is great served alongside cold meats or cheese, or as part of
a ploughman's lunch.

2 tablespoons olive oil

1.5 kg (3 lb) red (Spanish) onions,
   thinly sliced

2 cloves garlic, finely chopped

1 tablespoon mustard seeds

2 bay leaves

$^1/_2$ cup lightly packed brown sugar

1 cup white wine

1 cup white-wine vinegar

finely grated zest of 1 orange

juice of 2 oranges

Heat the oil in a large saucepan over low heat. Add the onion and garlic and cook, stirring occasionally, for 15 minutes, or until soft and lightly coloured. Add all the remaining ingredients, increase the heat and bring to the boil, stirring to dissolve the sugar. Reduce the heat and simmer, stirring frequently, until the mixture has reduced to a jam consistency – this will take 35–50 minutes.

Allow to cool, then spoon into sterilised screw-top jars and store in the refrigerator for up to 2 weeks.

Makes 3 cups

orange biscuits.

These biscuits are adapted from a recipe I found in a delightful old book titled *Kitchen Essays*, written by Agnes Jekyll (sister of the famed Victorian garden designer Gertrude Jekyll) in 1922.

125 g (4 oz) ground almonds (almond meal)
$^1/_2$ cup sugar
90 g (3 oz) butter

60 g (2 oz) plain (all-purpose) flour
grated zest and juice of 2 oranges

Preheat the oven to 180°C (350°F, Gas Mark 4). Line two oven trays with baking paper.

Place all the ingredients into a mixing bowl and beat with a wooden spoon until smooth and combined.

Using a tablespoon, scoop up small walnut-sized pieces of dough and place them on the prepared trays, leaving room for each to spread a little.

Bake for 8–10 minutes, or until firm and coloured. You may need to bake a third tray if any mixture remains. Cool on a wire rack.

Agnes's biscuits are delicious served with afternoon tea, or for dessert with ice-cream or to accompany a creamy dish.

Makes about 24

orange cordial.

Wonderfully refreshing on a hot summer's day, make this cordial in advance and have it chilled ready for use. The following gives you a concentrated syrup.

1^1/$_2$ cups caster (superfine) sugar
zest of ^{1}/$_2$ orange

juice of 6 oranges
juice of 2 lemons

Place the sugar and zest in a large heatproof bowl. Pour over 1½ cups of boiling water and stir until the sugar dissolves. Set aside to cool for 5 minutes.

Stir in the orange and lemon juice. Allow to cool to room temperature.

Strain the cordial into a jug or bottle, seal and store in the refrigerator for up to 7 days.

To serve, dilute 1 part syrup to 5 parts water, or to taste, and serve in tall glasses with plenty of ice. Garnish with fresh mint leaves and slices of lemon or orange.

Dilute the syrup with still or sparkling water.

Makes 3 cups concentrated syrup

orange poppy seed cake.

$^1/_2$ cup poppy seeds

$^3/_4$ cup milk

juice of $^1/_2$ lemon

250 g (8 oz) unsalted butter, softened

1 cup caster (superfine) sugar

grated zest of 1 orange

4 eggs

2 cups plain (all-purpose) flour

2 teaspoons baking powder

$^1/_2$ teaspoon bicarbonate of soda
   (sodium bicarbonate)

orange syrup (see below)

Soak the poppy seeds in the milk and lemon juice for 1–2 hours.

Preheat the oven to 180°C (350°F, Gas Mark 4). Lightly grease a 25 cm (10 in) kugelhopf or bundt cake tin.

Beat the butter, sugar and orange zest in an electric mixer until fluffy and pale. Beat in the eggs one at a time, alternating with a little flour, until combined. Sift together the remaining flour and the baking powder and bicarbonate of soda, then fold into the mixture. Gently stir in the milk mixture until smooth and combined.

Spoon the batter into the prepared tin. Bake for 55–60 minutes, or until the cake feels firms to the touch and a skewer inserted into the centre comes out clean. Allow to cool in the tin for 5 minutes, then turn out onto a large plate and brush hot orange syrup over the top and sides of the cake. Leave to cool.

To make the orange syrup, combine the juice from 2 oranges and ½ cup caster (superfine) sugar in a small saucepan. Bring to the boil over medium heat, stirring to dissolve the sugar, then simmer gently for 5 minutes.

orange semolina cake.

Semolina adds an interesting texture to cakes. This delicious version of orange cake keeps well and is good as a dessert or with a cup of tea.

125 g (4 oz) self-raising (self-rising) flour

1 teaspoon baking powder

1 1/2 cups semolina

1 cup caster (superfine) sugar

3 eggs, lightly beaten

200 ml (6 1/2 fl oz) plain natural yoghurt

1/2 cup milk

grated zest and juice of 1 orange

juice of 1/2 lemon

1/2 cup vegetable oil

orange syrup (see page 98)

Preheat the oven to 180°C (350°F, Gas Mark 4). Lightly grease a 23 cm (9 in) round cake tin and line the base with baking paper.

Sift the flour, baking powder, semolina and sugar into a large bowl and make a well in the centre.

In a separate bowl, combine the eggs, yoghurt, milk, orange zest and juice, lemon juice and oil. Pour the egg mixture into the flour mixture, stirring until just combined.

Pour the batter into the prepared tin. Bake for 40–45 minutes, or until firm to the touch and golden. A skewer inserted into the centre should come out clean. Allow to cool in the tin for 5 minutes, then turn out onto a large plate and brush the hot syrup over the top and sides of the cake. Leave to cool.

passionfruit ice-cream.

I love to see how a recipe changes as it travels from one person to the next. Many years ago I ate a delicious orange and cardamom ice-cream at Stephanie Alexander's restaurant in Melbourne. Gently flavoured and subtly spiced, the ice-cream was a revelation. Stephanie credited Jane Grigson (the great English food writer) with the recipe, who in turn had credited Jocelyn Dimbleby with the original. I have made it many times and in the process adapted the method to suit one of my favourite flavours – passionfruit.

8 passionfruit

175 g (6 oz) caster (superfine) sugar

3 large eggs

salt

300 ml ($9^1/_2$ fl oz) cream

Push the pulp from the passionfruit through a small sieve to remove the seeds, reserving 1 teaspoon of the seeds.

Place the sugar and 100 ml (3½ fl oz) of water in a small saucepan and bring to the boil, stirring to dissolve the sugar. Boil steadily for 3 minutes.

Meanwhile, beat the eggs and salt with an electric mixer until frothy.

Pour the sugar syrup into the egg mixture and continue to beat for 2–3 minutes, or until the mixture has thickened. Stir the sieved passionfruit and the reserved seeds into the mixture.

Lightly whip the cream and fold into the mixture. Churn in an ice-cream machine until frozen.

To make the original orange and cardamom version, follow the above but replace the passionfruit with ½ cup of concentrated orange juice and the crushed seeds from 5 cardamom pods.

Serves 6

passionfruit syllabub.

8 passionfruit

$^1/_3$ cup dessert wine

juice of $^1/_4$ lemon

50 g ($1^3/_4$ oz) caster (superfine) sugar

1 cup cream

Halve the passionfruit and scoop the pulp into a sieve set over a small bowl. Press on the pulp with the back of a spoon to extract all the juices. Reserve the juice and discard all but 1 teaspoon of the seeds.

Mix together the wine, lemon juice and sugar. Add the cream and whip the mixture slowly using a balloon whisk until soft peaks form. Fold in the passionfruit juice and the reserved seeds.

Spoon into four wine glasses and chill for 1 hour before serving.

Serves 4

pasta.

Fresh pasta is not difficult to make and is preferable to dried pasta when making lasagne and stuffed or filled pasta dishes. This version of pasta dough is adapted from Anna del Conte's recipe. A hand-cranked pasta machine will help enormously with the rolling and cutting.

220 g (7 oz) unbleached strong or plain (all-purpose) flour
1 teaspoon salt

2 large free-range or organic eggs, lightly beaten

Place the flour and salt in a food processor. With the processor running, add the eggs and process until the dough clumps together – it should be elastic but not moist. If necessary, add more flour.

Knead on a lightly floured surface for 5 minutes, or until smooth. Wrap in plastic wrap and leave at room temperature for 30 minutes.

Knead for a further 2 minutes, then divide the dough into four roughly equal pieces. Flatten each piece with your hand.

Set the pasta machine rollers to the thickest setting and run a piece of dough through the machine. Fold it in half, turn it 180 degrees and run it through again. Do this about 6 times. Change to the next-thickest setting and run the sheet of pasta through, then continue through every setting until the pasta is the desired thickness. You may have to dust the dough with flour occasionally, to stop it sticking. Repeat with the remaining pieces of dough.

For lasagne, ravioli or cannelloni, roll pasta through the thinnest setting and use immediately.

For spaghetti or tagliatelle, stop rolling at the second-last setting. Leave sheets to dry a little before cutting them.

Makes about 250 g

pasta with zucchini.

Simple pasta dishes are my staple fare. This one is especially easy, as the grated zucchini cooks quickly and can be prepared while the pasta cooks.

200 g (6^1/$_2$ oz) dried pasta

3 medium-sized zucchini (courgettes)

2 tablespoons olive oil

1 clove garlic, crushed

salt and freshly ground black pepper

2 tablespoons chopped flat-leaf parsley

^{1}/$_2$ cup freshly grated parmesan, plus extra to serve

extra-virgin olive oil, to serve

Bring a large saucepan of salted water to the boil and add the pasta. Stir well and boil rapidly until the pasta is al dente.

Meanwhile, grate the zucchini using the coarsest side of the grater, or cut the zucchini into thin strips.

Heat the olive oil in a frying pan over medium heat. Add the garlic and zucchini and cook, stirring, for about 5 minutes, or until the zucchini has released its juice and started to colour. Season well with salt and freshly ground black pepper.

Drain the cooked pasta and return it to the saucepan. Add the cooked zucchini and garlic, and the parsley and parmesan. Taste and adjust the seasoning. Serve drizzled with a little extra-virgin olive oil and extra grated parmesan.

I prefer thick spaghetti for this dish, and dried rather than fresh pasta.

As a variation you can replace some of the parsley with chopped rocket (arugula). You can also add some chopped prosciutto and a little chopped fresh chilli.

Serves 2

peach pie.

PASTRY

2 cups plain (all-purpose) flour

pinch of salt

125 g (4 oz) butter, chilled and diced

80–100 ml (2^3/$_4$–3^1/$_2$ fl oz) chilled water

FILLING

6 peaches

2 tablespoons demerara sugar or raw sugar

^{1}/$_3$ cup caster (superfine) sugar

2 egg yolks, lightly beaten

1 cup cream

To make the pastry, sift the flour and salt into a bowl. Rub the butter into the flour mixture with your fingertips until it resembles coarse breadcrumbs. Make a well in the centre, add the water and mix until the mixture just comes together, adding extra water if needed. Gently press the pastry into a ball and flatten slightly. Wrap in plastic wrap and refrigerate for 30 minutes.

Grease a 25 cm (10 in) loose-based tart tin.

Roll out the pastry between two sheets of baking paper, until large enough to line the base and sides of the tin. Line the tin with pastry, allowing any excess to hang over the sides. Chill for 15 minutes.

Preheat the oven to 200°C (400°F, Gas Mark 5.)

Halve, stone and peel the peaches. Slice each half into four and line the pastry case with peaches. Sprinkle with the demerara sugar. Bake for 15 minutes. Remove from the heat and reduce the oven to 150°C (300°F, Gas Mark 2).

Lightly beat the caster sugar, egg yolks and cream together and pour over the peaches. Return the pie to the oven for 25–30 minutes, or until the custard is set. Trim the edges and serve warm.

Nectarines work well in this pie in place of the peaches.

Serves 8

peanut biscuits.

125 g (4 oz) unsalted butter, chopped and softened

$^1/_2$ cup lightly packed brown sugar

1 cup self-raising (self-rising) flour

1 cup roasted salted peanuts

2 tablespoons strong coffee, freshly made

Preheat the oven to 180°C (350°F, Gas Mark 4). Grease two oven trays and line with baking paper.

Place the butter in a medium-sized mixing bowl and add the sugar. Beat with an electric mixer for 2–3 minutes, or until smooth and fluffy. Sift in the flour and add the peanuts and coffee. Mix with a wooden spoon until combined.

Roll tablespoons of the mixture into balls and place on the prepared trays, leaving 5 cm (2 in) between each to allow for spreading. Flatten each ball with your thumb or the back of a fork.

Bake for 10–12 minutes, or until golden. Remove from the oven and allow to cool on the trays for 5 minutes, then transfer to wire racks to cool completely. Store in an airtight container for up to 1 week.

Use salted or unsalted peanuts depending on your preference. If using unsalted peanuts, add a pinch of salt to the mixture with the flour.

Makes about 24

piri piri sauce.

Piri Piri is the variety of chilli used to create this hot and spicy sauce. Piri Piri sauce is the key ingredient in the well-loved dish Portuguese chicken.

6 long red chillies, seeded
3 cloves garlic, crushed

juice of 1 lemon
¹/₂ cup olive oil

Place all the ingredients in a food processor and process until smooth. Store the sauce in an airtight container in the refrigerator for up to 5 days.

To make Portuguese chicken, cut a small chicken down the backbone with a sharp knife or scissors and press down on the breastbone to flatten it. Season lightly with salt and freshly ground black pepper. Brush the chicken well with Piri Piri sauce. Cover and refrigerate for at least 3 hours (or overnight). Cook the chicken skin-side down on a hot, ribbed grill pan, or a heavy frying pan, until golden, then transfer to a preheated 200°C (400°F, Gas Mark 6) oven and cook skin-side up for 35–40 minutes, or until nicely coloured and cooked. Serve accompanied with lemon wedges.

I use long red chillies for the sauce, but if you like your food really hot you can substitute a few short chillies for the longer, milder varieties.

Makes ¾ cup

pizza bianca.

In this recipe my basic pizza dough is brushed with olive oil, sprinkled with garlic and rosemary, and topped with mozarella – the simplest of all pizza toppings.

1 × 7 g ($^1/_4$ oz) sachet (2 teaspoons) dry
    yeast
1 teaspoon sugar
2$^1/_2$ cups bread flour
salt

100 ml olive oil
3 cloves garlic, crushed
2 teaspoons roughly chopped rosemary
1 tablespoon sea salt
1 × 200 g (6$^1/_2$ oz) mozzarella ball, sliced

Dissolve the yeast and sugar in a small bowl with 200 ml (6½ fl oz) of tepid water. Stir well and set aside for 10 minutes, or until the mixture froths.

Place the flour and a pinch of salt in a large mixing bowl. Make a well in the centre and add the yeast mixture and 2 tablespoons of the olive oil. Mix until a firm dough forms.

Knead on a lightly floured surface for 5–7 minutes, or until smooth and elastic. Place in a clean, lightly oiled bowl, cover with plastic wrap and leave in a warm place for 1–1½ hours, or until the dough has doubled in size.

Preheat the oven to 220°C (425°F, Gas Mark 7).

Place the garlic and rosemary in a small bowl with the remaining oil.

Punch down the dough with your fist to release the air. Divide into two equal portions and roll out or press to a thickness of 4–5 mm (¼ in). Transfer to lightly oiled pizza trays.

Brush with the rosemary mixture and sprinkle with sea salt. Top with sliced mozzarella. Cook for 20 minutes, or until crisp underneath and molten on top.

Makes 2 × 30 cm (12 in) pizza bases

pizza margherita.

cornmeal or polenta, to sprinkle

1 quantity homemade basic pizza dough
(see page 111), or 2 bought pizza bases

1 cup tomato pizza sauce, homemade (see
below) or bought

2 × 150 g (5 oz) mozzarella balls, cut into
thin rounds

$^1/_4$ cup extra-virgin olive oil, plus extra,
to serve

salt and freshly ground black pepper

12 small basil leaves

Lightly oil two 30 cm (12 in) pizza trays or oven trays and sprinkle with a little cornmeal.

Make the basic pizza dough as described on page 111. After the first rise, punch down the dough with your fist to expel the air and gently knead for 1 minute. Divide the dough into two portions. Roll each portion into a 30 cm (12 in) diameter circle.

Preheat the oven to 240°C (465°F, Gas Mark 9).

Transfer the pizza bases to the prepared trays. Spread each base with an even layer of tomato sauce. Top with the mozzarella slices and drizzle with the extra-virgin olive oil. Season well with salt and freshly ground black pepper.

Bake for 12–15 minutes, or until the base is golden and the cheese has melted. Remove from the oven, drizzle with a little extra oil and scatter over the basil.

To make an easy tomato pizza sauce, strain 2 × 400 g (13 oz) cans of chopped or crushed toma-
toes in a fine sieve for about 10 minutes, discarding the liquid. Place the tomato flesh, 2 cloves of
crushed garlic, ¼ cup of olive oil and ½ teaspoon of dried oregano in a medium-sized saucepan
and cook over low heat, stirring frequently, for 20–30 minutes, or until thick. Season to taste with
salt and freshly ground black pepper. Store in a sealed container in the refrigerator for up to 5 days,
or freeze for up to 2 months.

Makes 2 × 30 cm (12 in) pizzas

poached cherries.

This is a delicious way to preserve the last of the summer cherries.

500 g (1 lb) cherries

3 cups red wine

1^1/$_2$ cups caster (superfine) sugar

1 cinnamon stick

2 tablespoons redcurrant jelly

2 tablespoons brandy (optional)

Remove the stems from the cherries and place the cherries in a medium-sized sauce-pan. Pour over the red wine, making sure there is enough wine to cover the fruit – add extra if needed. Add the sugar and cinnamon stick. Bring the mixture slowly to the boil, stirring frequently to dissolve the sugar. Cover and simmer gently over low heat for 10 minutes. Remove the saucepan from the heat and set aside to cool.

Drain the cherries, reserving the syrup. Discard the cinnamon.

Sterilize two medium-sized screw-top jars by filling them with boiling water. Drain them on a clean tea towel.

Divide the cherries between the jars.

Bring the syrup back to the boil and simmer until the liquid has reduced by one third. Remove from the heat. Stir in the redcurrant jelly and brandy and pour over the cherries. Seal the jars and set aside to cool.

Store in the refrigerator for up to 2 months. Once opened, use the cherries within 7 days. The cherries and syrup are delicious served with vanilla ice-cream.

For the wine, use a light, Italian-style red wine or a pinot noir.

Choose cherries that are plump and shiny and have green stalks

I never bother stoning cherries, but cherry stoners are available in kitchenware shops if you prefer no pips.

Makes 1 litre

pommes anna.

This delicious, golden and crispy potato cake is perfect with just about anything (think roast chicken, lamb or beef, or steak).

1.35 kg (2 lb 11 oz) potatoes, peeled and thinly sliced	**50 g (1³/₄ oz) butter**
	salt and freshly ground black pepper

Preheat the oven to 200°C (400°F, Gas Mark 6).

Melt the butter over medium heat in a 20 cm (8 in) heavy-based frying pan with an ovenproof handle. Remove from the heat and place the potato slices in a single overlapping layer on the bottom of the pan. Season with salt and freshly ground black pepper. Repeat the layering process with the rest of the potato, seasoning each layer as you go. You should end up with potato to a depth of 3 cm (1¼ in).

Return the frying pan to the heat and cook for 1–2 minutes, to colour the potatoes. Cover with foil, transfer to the oven and bake for 30 minutes. Remove foil and cook for a further 30 minutes, or until the potatoes are golden and a sharp knife is easily inserted into their centres. Remove from the oven and let sit for 5 minutes, then invert the potato cake onto a serving plate. Cut into wedges.

I use desiree potatoes for this dish.

Serves 6

pork satays.

1 kg (2 lb) pork fillet	1 clove garlic, chopped
salt and freshly ground black pepper	2 tablespoons soy sauce
$^1/_4$ cup vegetable oil	juice of 1 lime
1 teaspoon grated fresh ginger	satay sauce (see page 138)
1 long red chilli, finely chopped	3 small red onions, each cut into eighths

Cut the pork fillet into 2 cm (¾ in) cubes and season lightly with salt and freshly ground black pepper.

Combine the oil, ginger, chilli, garlic, soy sauce and lime juice in a bowl. Add the pork pieces and mix well. Cover and allow to marinate in the refrigerator for at least 2 hours (but no longer than 4 hours).

If using bamboo skewers, soak them in water for 30 minutes.

Thread the pork onto the skewers alternating with the onion pieces.

Preheat a ribbed grill pan or heavy frying pan over high heat. Add the skewers and cook for 10 minutes, turning once or twice.

Meanwhile, heat the satay sauce in a small saucepan. Serve two skewers per person accompanied with the warmed sauce.

Serves 4

portuguese custard tarts.

8 egg yolks

2 eggs

$^1/_2$ cup caster (superfine) sugar

1 tablespoon plain (all-purpose) flour

$^1/_2$ teaspoon finely grated orange zest

1 × 380 g (12 oz) packet frozen puff
   pastry, thawed

1 teaspoon ground cinnamon

2 teaspoons caster (superfine) sugar, for
   sprinkling, plus extra for rolling

icing (confectioners') sugar, to serve
   (optional)

Place the yolks, eggs, sugar, flour and orange zest in a bowl and beat with a whisk or
hand-held beater for about 3 minutes, or until the mixture is pale and thick. Transfer to
a small saucepan and place over low heat, stirring, until the mixture has thickened –
do not let it boil. Allow to cool.

Roll out the pastry to a size approximately 20 cm (8 in) square.

Combine the cinnamon and the 2 teaspoons of caster sugar and sprinkle over the
pastry. Roll up tightly to form a log. Wrap in plastic wrap and chill for 30 minutes.

Lightly grease a 12-cup muffin tin.

Cut the pastry log into discs 1.5 cm ($^5/_8$ in) wide. Lightly dust a work surface with
caster sugar, then roll the discs until each is 11 cm (4½ in) in diameter. Press each pastry
circle into a cup of the muffin tin. Chill for 15 minutes.

Meanwhile, preheat the oven to 220°C (425°F, Gas Mark 7). Transfer the custard to
a jug and fill each pastry cup three-quarters full. Bake for 15 minutes, or until the custard has coloured and the pastry is golden. (The custard filling may rise while cooking,
but will sink again when cool.) Eat warm or cold, dusted with icing sugar if desired.

Makes 12

prawn cocktail.

24 medium-to-large cooked prawns
    (shrimp)
1 small iceberg lettuce
1 lemon, quartered, to serve

COCKTAIL SAUCE
1 cup good-quality mayonnaise (preferably
    homemade)

$^1/_3$ cup tomato sauce (ketchup)
1 tablespoon Worcestershire sauce
1 tablespoon brandy
1 tablespoon lemon juice
$^1/_4$ cup cream, whipped
salt and freshly ground black pepper

Peel and devein the prawns, leaving on the tails, if desired.

Remove and discard any broken or limp outer leaves from the lettuce and cut it into four wedges with a sharp knife.

Make the cocktail sauce by combining the mayonnaise, tomato sauce, Worcestershire sauce, brandy and lemon juice. Stir in the whipped cream. Season with salt and freshly ground black pepper and adjust the quantities of the other ingredients to suit your taste.

To serve, place a wedge of lettuce on each plate, spoon over some sauce and surround with six prawns. Serve with a wedge of lemon.

I like to use fresh, ready-cooked prawns for this dish — they are usually cooked on the trawler in salt water, giving them a good flavour.

Add a drop or two of Tabasco sauce to the cocktail sauce if you like a little spice.

Serves 4

prawn toasts.

250 g (8 oz) uncooked prawns (shrimp),
   shelled and deveined
1 egg white
2 spring onions (scallions), chopped
1 teaspoon grated fresh ginger
1 tablespoon roughly chopped coriander
   (cilantro) leaves

1 tablespoon cornflour (cornstarch)
6 slices white bread
$^1/_3$ cup sesame seeds
vegetable oil, for frying

Roughly chop the prawns and place in a food processor with the egg white, spring onion, ginger, coriander and cornflour. Process using the pulse action until just combined but still a little chunky.

Spread each slice of bread evenly with the prawn mixture. Sprinkle generously with the sesame seeds. Trim the crusts off the bread and cut each slice into quarters.

Pour the oil into a large frying pan to a depth of 1 cm (½ in). Heat over medium heat to 180°C (350°F), or until a cube of bread dropped into the oil browns in about 20 seconds. Fry the toasts in batches, starting with the side spread with the prawn mixture face down and cooking for about 10 seconds. Turn the toasts and cook for a further 10 seconds, or until golden and crisp. Repeat with remaining toasts. Drain on kitchen paper and serve immediately.

Makes 24

quiche lorraine.

A homemade quiche, with its crisp pastry and slightly wobbly centre,
is a great dish – it wins hands down over any store-bought counterpart.

1 quantity homemade shortcrust pastry (see
    page 106), or 1 × 380 g (12 oz) packet
    bought frozen shortcrust pastry, thawed
5 rashers streaky bacon, diced
100 g (3¹/₂ oz) gruyere cheese, grated

³/₄ cup cream
¹/₂ cup milk
¹/₂ teaspoon Dijon mustard
3 eggs, lightly beaten
salt and freshly ground black pepper

Prepare the pastry according to the instructions on page 106 and refrigerate for at least 30 minutes before using.

Roll out the pastry between two sheets of baking paper to a size to fit a 23 cm (9 in) deep, fluted flan tin. Grease the tin. Line the tin with the pastry, pressing it into the edges. Trim any excess pastry. Chill for 30 minutes.

Preheat the oven to 190°C (375°F, Gas Mark 5).

Line the pastry case with foil or baking paper. Half-fill the pastry case with pie weights, uncooked dried beans or rice and bake for 15 minutes. Remove the weights and foil and bake the pastry case for a further 10 minutes, or until dry and lightly coloured.

Reduce the oven temperature to 170°C (325°F, Gas Mark 3).

Place the bacon in a small frying pan over medium heat and cook, stirring, until crisp. Sprinkle over the pastry case, along with the gruyere cheese.

Whisk the cream, milk, mustard and eggs in a bowl until smooth. Season well with salt and freshly ground black pepper. Pour into the pastry case and bake for 35–40 minutes, or until just set. Serve warm.

Serves 6

quick flaky pastry.

This pastry is useful for covering a meat or other savoury pie.

300 g (9^1/$_2$ oz) plain (all-purpose) flour
salt

175 g (6 oz) butter, frozen for 30 minutes
before use
80–100 ml (2^3/$_4$–3^1/$_2$ fl oz) chilled water

Sift the flour and a pinch of salt into a large bowl. Using the largest holes of a grater, grate the frozen butter into the flour. Gently mix with a knife or flat spatula, making sure that all the pieces of butter are coated in flour – the butter should be left in chunky grated pieces, not worked into the dough.

Add about 80 ml (2¾ fl oz) of the chilled water to the flour and butter mixture and mix in with the spatula. The pastry should come together in clumps – add a little extra water if necessary. When the dough holds together, roll it into a ball and flatten slightly to form a disc. Cover with plastic wrap and refrigerate for at least 30 minutes before using.

It is important to use frozen butter and to handle the dough as little as possible.

Any leftover pastry can be placed in a freezer bag and frozen for up to 2 months.

Makes enough to cover a 28 cm (11 in) pie dish

quick indian-style lamb curry.

1 cup plain natural yoghurt

juice of 1 lemon

2 teaspoons cornflour (cornstarch)

2 cloves garlic, crushed

1 teaspoon grated fresh ginger

1 kg (2 lb) shoulder or leg of lamb, trimmed
  and cubed

2 tablespoons vegetable oil

1 onion, finely chopped

1 tablespoon curry powder (see page 46)

1 × 400 g (13 oz) can chopped tomatoes

2 tablespoons tomato paste

1 long red chilli, seeded and finely chopped

$^1/_2$ cup beef stock or water

$^1/_2$ teaspoon salt

1 bay leaf

salt, extra, and freshly ground black pepper

$^1/_2$ cup coarsely chopped coriander
  (cilantro) leaves

In a large bowl, combine the yoghurt, lemon juice, cornflour, garlic and ginger. Add the lamb pieces and toss to coat thoroughly. Cover and allow to marinate in the refrigerator overnight.

Heat the oil in a large saucepan over medium heat and sauté the onion for 4–5 minutes, or until golden. Add the curry powder and cook, stirring, for 2 minutes. Add the lamb and its marinade to the saucepan and cook, stirring, for 10 minutes. Stir in the tomatoes, tomato paste, chilli, stock, salt and bay leaf. Cover and simmer over gentle heat for 1½–2 hours, or until the meat is tender. Taste and add extra curry powder, if desired. Add extra water or stock if the sauce becomes too thick during cooking.

Season to taste with salt and freshly ground black pepper and stir in the coriander. Serve with steamed rice.

Serves 4–6

raspberry cordial.

Raspberries can make a delicious soft drink for the summer season. The following recipe gives you a concentrated base.

300 g (9^1/$_2$ oz) raspberries, fresh, or frozen
    and thawed
1^1/$_4$ cups caster (superfine) sugar

juice of 5 lemons
lemon slices, to serve
sprigs of mint, to serve

Place the raspberries and sugar in a blender and pulse until smooth. Strain through a sieve into a large bowl. Add the lemon juice and stir until well mixed and the sugar has dissolved.

Transfer the mixture to a large bottle or storage container and refrigerate for up to 5 days. Dilute with still or sparkling water, as desired. Serve with ice, slices of lemon and a sprig of mint.

As a variation, replace the raspberries with an equal quantity of strawberries.

To give it a little kick, try this cordial with a dash of gin or vodka, and dilute it with soda or mineral water.

Makes 3 cups concentrated syrup

raspberry sundae.

A sundae is fun to make and a great way to get the kids into the kitchen.
This simple dessert is more about assembling ingredients than
cooking and is the perfect treat in hot weather.

2 cups good-quality vanilla ice-cream

250 g (8 oz) strawberries, hulled

200 g (6¹/₂ oz) fresh raspberries

SAUCE

1 teaspoon lemon juice

200 g (6¹/₂ oz) raspberries, fresh, or frozen
   and thawed

2 teaspoons icing (confectioners') sugar,
   sifted

Make the raspberry sauce first. Blend the lemon juice, raspberries and icing sugar in an electric blender until smooth. (This mixture may be made ahead of time and chilled until ready to use.)

Transfer the ice-cream to the refrigerator 15–20 minutes before serving, to allow it to soften slightly.

Halve the strawberries, if large.

When ready to assemble, place a large scoop of ice-cream in the base of four sundae glasses. Top with a few berries, then drizzle over a layer of raspberry sauce. Continue layering until the glasses are almost full, finishing by drizzling the raspberry sauce over the top. Serve immediately.

This sundae is even better if you add a layer of roughly chopped or crushed meringues between the layers of fruit.

Use any combination of ripe fruit and good-quality ice-cream that you like.

Makes 4

risotto with sausage and red wine.

1.35 litres (43 fl oz) chicken stock, beef
    stock or veal stock
60 g (2 oz) butter
1 onion, chopped
400 g (13 oz) good-quality Italian-style
    sausages, skinned

1 cup arborio or Carnaroli rice
$^1/_2$ cup robust red wine
handful of flat-leaf parsley, chopped
$^3/_4$ cup freshly grated parmesan, plus extra
    to serve
salt and freshly ground black pepper

Bring the stock to a gentle simmer in a large saucepan.

Meanwhile, melt 40 g (1½ oz) of the butter in a large, heavy-based saucepan over medium heat. Add the onion and cook, stirring, for 3 minutes, or until soft. Increase the heat a little and add the sausage meat. Cook, stirring, until the meat colours, breaking up any lumps with a fork. Add the rice and stir gently for 2 minutes. Add the wine. Stir and allow most of the liquid to evaporate.

Add enough of the simmering stock to just cover the rice. Stirring frequently, allow the rice to absorb most of the stock. Repeat the process, stirring well and adding stock as required. (If the stock runs out before the rice is cooked, continue with simmering water.) It will take 18–25 minutes to cook. Taste the rice for texture – it should be soft but still retain a little bite.

Remove from the heat and add the parsley, parmesan and the remaining butter. Season to taste with salt and freshly ground black pepper. Cover and allow to rest for 5 minutes before serving. Serve with extra grated parmesan, if desired.

Serves 4

roast beetroot.

There is much more to beetroot than the vinegary purple slices you find in cans (where would an Aussie burger be without the stuff?) Give yourself a treat and try the delicious sweetness of roasted fresh beetroot.

6–8 small beetroots

2 tablespoons olive oil

salt and freshly ground black pepper

Preheated the oven to 180°C (350°F, Gas Mark 4).

Trim the tops of the beetroots, leaving a little of the stem attached, but don't peel them. Halve any large ones, and place them all in a baking tin. Drizzle with a little of the olive oil and cover with foil. Roast for 1½–2 hours, or until beetroot is tender when pierced with a skewer or sharp knife.

Allow to cool a little, then slip the skins off the beetroots and halve or quarter them. Drizzle with the remaining olive oil, or toss with butter or sour cream and herbs while hot. Season with salt and freshly ground black pepper.

Serve hot as a side dish or at room temperature as part of a salad.

Look for a bunch of small-to-medium-sized beetroots that has firm, nicely coloured flesh and fresh leaves.

If short of time, you can parboil the beetroots before roasting, then reduce the roasting time to 30 minutes.

Hot beetroots are also delicious dressed with balsamic vinegar and olive oil and sprinkled with fresh chives.

Serves 4–6

roast fish in paper.

4 snapper, blue-eye cod, jewfish or other
    firm white fish fillets
sea salt and freshly ground black pepper
8 thin slices of lemon

1 tablespoon chopped chives
8 mint leaves, roughly chopped
30 g (1 oz) butter
1 lemon, quartered, to serve

Preheat the oven to 200°C (400°F, Gas Mark 6).

Cut four sheets of baking paper 35 cm (14 in) square. Place one sheet on your work surface and place a fish fillet to the right of centre of the paper, narrow end towards you. Season the fillet well with salt and freshly ground black pepper and top with two slices of lemon. Sprinkle with some of the herbs and add a small knob of the butter.

Fold over the left half of the paper to enclose the fish and then fold the remaining two edges over twice to seal well, making a tight parcel. My mum used wooden pegs or sometimes paper clips to seal the parcel (remove before serving). Lift the parcel onto an oven tray. Repeat with the remaining fillets, leaving space on the oven tray between each parcel.

Bake for 12–15 minutes – the paper parcel should puff up a little. Transfer the parcels to serving plates so they can be opened at the table. Serve with lemon quarters and a crisp, green salad.

Serves 4

roast pears.

4 ripe pears

2 tablespoons golden syrup

chopped zest of 1 lime

$^1/_2$ cup lightly packed brown sugar

Preheat the oven to 180°C (350°F, Gas Mark 4).

Halve the pears lengthways, leaving the skin on, and scoop out the cores. Place the pears cut-side up in a baking tin.

Combine 1 cup of water and the golden syrup, lime zest and sugar in a small saucepan and bring to the boil. Cool slightly, then pour the syrup over the pears.

Roast, turning and basting occasionally, for 45–50 minutes, or until tender and nicely golden. If the syrup starts to dry up during cooking, add a little hot water to the dish.

Serve pears warm or at room temperature, drizzled with the pan juices and accompanied by a generous spoonful of yoghurt, ice-cream or cream.

Beurre bosc pears are ideal for this dish.

As a variation, sprinkle the pears with a little ground ginger, cinnamon or cardamom before roasting.

Serves 4

salade niçoise.

There really are as many recipes – and rules – for a salade niçoise as there are cooks. It is always a simple and delicious dish, though, and the combination of flavours has travelled well from the south of France to the southern hemisphere. Vary the recipe with ingredients that you have to hand, but here is my basic version.

4 eggs

1 cos (Romaine) lettuce

5 ripe tomatoes, cut into wedges

100 g ($3^1/_2$ oz) small black olives

350 g (11 oz) small new or salad potatoes, freshly boiled and halved

250 g (8 oz) green beans, freshly boiled

100 ml ($3^1/_2$ fl oz) good-quality olive oil

2 tablespoons lemon juice

1 teaspoon Dijon mustard

1 × 250 g (8 oz) can tuna in oil, drained

1 teaspoon capers

6–8 anchovy fillets

salt and freshly ground black pepper

Hard-boil the eggs in a saucepan of boiling water for 7 minutes. Set aside until cool, then peel and quarter.

To assemble the salad, trim, wash and dry the lettuce and break the leaves into largish pieces. Combine with the tomatoes, olives, potatoes and beans.

Make a dressing by mixing together the olive oil, lemon juice and mustard.

Lightly dress the salad and transfer to a serving plate. Top with the eggs and the tuna. Sprinkle over the capers and top with the anchovy fillets. Drizzle with a little extra dressing and season well with salt and freshly ground black pepper.

Use good-quality canned tuna. Alternatively, sear four small tuna steaks in a frying pan over high heat for about 2 minutes each side and serve them with the salad.

Serves 4

salt-baked prawns.

This is a simple but very effective way to cook raw prawns – baking them in salt
seals the prawns completely so they cook without any juice or flavour escaping.
The idea comes from a friend I met at the Sydney Seafood Cooking School.

1 kg (2 lb) coarse rock salt
8 sprigs thyme
4 cloves garlic, skin on

24 medium-sized uncooked prawns
(shrimp), shells on
1 bay leaf
lemon wedges, to serve
mayonnaise, to serve

Preheat the oven to 220°C (425°F, Gas Mark 7).

Place half the rock salt in a 1 cm (½ in) layer on the base of a small baking tin.
Lay half the thyme and half the garlic on the salt and add the prawns. Sprinkle over
the remaining thyme and garlic and add the bay leaf, then cover completely with the
remaining salt. Sprinkle lightly with a couple of tablespoons of water. Bake for 10–12
minutes.

Crack the salt and remove the prawns – this can be done at the table, if desired.

Serve with lemon wedges and accompany with good-quality mayonnaise.

The salt can be saved and reused to make this dish again.

Serves 4

san choy bow.

1 tablespoon peanut oil

1 onion, finely chopped

1 clove garlic, crushed

2 teaspoons grated fresh ginger

600 g (1¹/₄ lb) minced (ground) pork

1 tablespoon soy sauce

2 tablespoons oyster sauce

1 × 220 g (7 oz) can water chestnuts,
     drained and chopped

4 spring onions (scallions), thinly sliced

salt and freshly ground black pepper

250 g (8 oz) bean sprouts

8 iceberg lettuce leaves

Heat the oil in a large frying pan over medium heat. Cook the onion, garlic and ginger, stirring occasionally, for 3–4 minutes, or until the onion is soft. Add the minced pork and cook, breaking up the meat with a fork, for 4–5 minutes, or until the pork is coloured and cooked. Stir in the soy sauce, oyster sauce, water chestnuts and spring onion and cook for a further 3–4 minutes, or until the liquid has reduced. Season to taste with salt and pepper.

Transfer the mixture to a bowl and stir in the bean sprouts. Allow to cool slightly before serving. Place two lettuce leaves on each serving plate and spoon the mixture into the centre of the leaves. Serve immediately.

This recipe is just as good using minced (ground) chicken instead of pork.

Serves 4

satay sauce.

2 tablespoons vegetable oil

1 onion, finely chopped

2 cloves garlic, crushed

1 teaspoon grated fresh ginger

1–2 long red chillies, finely chopped

1 tablespoon brown sugar

$^1/_2$ cup crunchy peanut butter

juice of 1 lime

1 teaspoon Thai fish sauce

2 tablespoons soy sauce

salt and freshly ground black pepper

Heat the oil in a saucepan over medium heat. Add the onion, garlic, ginger and chilli and cook, stirring, for 4–5 minutes, or until the onion is soft. Add the sugar, peanut butter, lime juice, fish sauce, soy sauce and 2–3 tablespoons of water. Simmer gently for 5 minutes, adding a little extra water if needed, to produce a sauce-like consistency. Taste and add a little extra lime juice or fish sauce, if desired. Season to taste with salt and freshly ground pepper.

Store in an airtight container in the refrigerator for up to 1 week.

Add 1 teaspoon of crushed dried chillies, if desired, for extra heat.

Makes about 1 cup

sausage roast.

This delicious recipe comes from my friend and great cook Fiona Beckett.
If you want a supper that calls for minimal effort but is very, very soothing
and comforting, make this.

450 g (14 oz) new or waxy potatoes

2 red (Spanish) onions

4 cloves garlic or a head of 'wet'
(fresh) garlic

$^1/_4$ cup olive oil

salt and freshly ground black pepper

6 good-quality lamb and mint or
lamb and rosemary sausages

Preheat the oven to 200°C (400°F, Gas Mark 6).

Scrub the potatoes clean but don't peel them. Cut into chunky slices about 4–5 cm
(1½–2 in) thick.

Peel and thickly slice the onions and garlic. Place in a medium-sized baking tin with
the potatoes and pour over the oil. Season with salt and pepper, then toss to coat well
with the oil and seasonings.

Roast for 20 minutes. Remove from the oven and turn the vegetables. Lay the
sausages on top of the vegetables, turning them so they get a light coating of oil. Roast
for 20 minutes, then turn the sausages over and cook for a further 15–20 minutes.

I don't think this is a dish that needs gravy, but if you're a gravy addict, feel free.
Serve it with a classic French-style green salad.

Buy good-quality sausages, with a high meat content, from your local butcher.

*This dish can be easily doubled to serve 4–6. Use either one large baking tin or two smaller
tins, swapping their position in the oven halfway through the cooking.*

Serves 2

singapore-style noodles.

250 g (8 oz) rice vermicelli (cellophane)
  noodles
2 large red chillies, seeded and roughly
  chopped
3 cloves garlic, crushed
1 × $\frac{1}{2}$ cm ($\frac{1}{4}$ in) piece fresh ginger,
  chopped
1 small onion, roughly chopped
$\frac{1}{4}$ cup vegetable oil

2 chicken breasts, thinly sliced
12 uncooked prawns (shrimp), shelled and
  deveined
1 cup bean sprouts
4 spring onions (scallions), sliced
1 egg, beaten
$\frac{1}{4}$ cup light soy sauce
juice of $\frac{1}{2}$ lemon or lime
salt

Place the noodles in a heatproof bowl and cover with boiling water. Leave to soften for 7 minutes. Drain well and set aside.

Place the chilli, garlic, ginger and onion in a food processor. Use the pulse action to process ingredients to a paste, adding a drizzle of vegetable oil if needed. Alternatively, pound ingredients to a paste in a mortar and pestle.

Heat a wok or large frying pan to hot, then add the vegetable oil, turning to coat the pan. Add the paste and cook, stirring, for 30 seconds – be careful it does not burn.

Add the chicken and stir-fry for 2–3 minutes. Add the prawns and stir-fry for a further minute, or until the chicken is golden and the prawns are cooked. Add the drained noodles and the bean sprouts, spring onions and egg and cook, stirring continuously, for 2 minutes. Pour over the soy sauce and continue to cook and stir until combined and hot. Squeeze over a little lemon or lime juice and season to taste with salt.

Try 250 g (8 oz) of sliced fresh pork fillet in place of the chicken.

Serves 3–4

slow-roasted lamb.

Slow cooking gives you wonderfully succulent and tender meat. Use a medium-sized leg of lamb or get your butcher to bone and roll a large shoulder of lamb.

2 tablespoons vegetable oil

1 medium-sized leg or rolled shoulder
    of lamb

4 rashers bacon or pancetta, chopped

1 onion, chopped

2 cloves garlic, peeled

1 bay leaf

3 sprigs rosemary or thyme

$1–1^{1}/_{3}$ cups red wine

salt and freshly ground black pepper

Preheat the oven to 200°C (400°F, Gas Mark 6).

Heat the oil in a large casserole dish or deep baking tin over medium heat and brown the lamb on both sides. Remove the lamb, add the bacon and cook, stirring occasionally, for 3 minutes. Add the onion and cook for a further 4–5 minutes, or until tender. Return the lamb to the casserole and add the garlic, bay leaf and rosemary. Pour in the red wine to a depth of about 1 cm (½ in) and bring to the boil.

Cover the casserole with a lid or sheet of foil and place in the oven. Reduce the heat to 160°C (315°F, Gas Mark 2–3) and cook for 4–4½ hours, or until the meat is very tender, turning the lamb and basting occasionally.

Remove the lamb from the dish, cover with foil and allow to rest for 10 minutes before carving.

Skim off any fat from the surface of the pan with a large spoon and remove the garlic, bay leaf and rosemary. If the sauce is a little thin, reduce it over high heat on the stove top. Season to taste with salt and freshly ground black pepper.

Slice the meat and serve with the sauce.

Serves 4–6

slow-roasted pork.

This recipe is from Nigella Lawson's book *Nigella Bites*. 'I do like the sort of cooking that gets on with itself slowly,' she says. Many a Sunday lunch at my home starts with thanks to Nigella.

A point before you start – this dish does take 24 hours to cook, but for most of that time you ignore it completely (and it does make the kitchen smell like something wonderfully delicious is going on).

6 cloves garlic, peeled and chopped	2 tablespoons olive oil
1 × 1 cm (¹/₂ in) piece fresh ginger, peeled and chopped	3–4 tablespoons sherry or rice vinegar
	1 × 3–4 kg (6–8 lbs) shoulder pork
2 long red chillies, chopped	2 tablespoons olive oil, extra, to serve

Preheat the oven to 240°C (475°F, Gas Mark 9).

Pound the garlic, ginger, chillies and oil with enough vinegar in a mortar and pestle to form a paste. Alternatively, process the ingredients in a small food processor.

Score the skin of the pork by cutting it in several places with a knife – be careful not to cut all the way through. Rub the chilli paste all over the top of the pork, including deep into the scored skin.

Place the pork, scored-side up, on a roasting rack set over a baking tin. Roast for 30 minutes. Remove from the oven and reduce the heat to 120°C (250°F, Gas Mark ½). Turn the pork over so the scoring is underneath. Bake for 23 hours.

Prior to serving, turn the oven up to the highest setting, turn the pork skin-side up and cook for 30 mintues, or until the crackling is crisp. To serve, slice away the crackling and carve the meat into large pieces.

Serves 6–8

spaghetti vongole.

You can prepare the clams (vongole) and make the sauce in the time
it takes to cook the spaghetti.

2 tablespoons olive oil

2 cloves garlic, crushed

1 long red chilli, chopped

200 g (6^1/$_2$ oz) cherry tomatoes, halved

750 g (1^1/$_2$ lb) fresh clams (vongole)

200 g (6^1/$_2$ oz) dried spaghetti

2–3 tablespoons chopped flat-leaf parsley

salt and freshly ground black pepper

1 lemon, quartered, to serve

Put a large saucepan of salted water on to boil.

Pour the oil into a second large saucepan over moderate heat. Add the garlic and chilli and sauté for 2–3 minutes. Add the tomatoes and cook for 1–2 minutes, or until soft. Tip in the clams and stir well. Increase the heat, cover and cook, shaking the pan occasionally, for 5–6 minutes, or until the clams have opened.

Meanwhile, cook the spaghetti in the boiling water until al dente.

Drain the pasta and add it to the saucepan containing the clams. Sprinkle with the parsley and toss the pasta and clams together well. Season to taste with salt and freshly ground black pepper – the juices that clams release when they cook can be salty, so taste first. Serve in large bowls with lemon wedges.

Cleaned mussels may be substituted for the clams.

Serves 2

spaghetti with crab and chilli.

200 g (6$^1/_2$ oz) dried spaghetti

200 g (6$^1/_2$ oz) fresh cooked crab meat, white or brown

$^1/_2$ long red chilli, seeded and finely sliced

1 clove garlic, crushed

1 teaspoon grated lemon zest

handful of rocket (arugula), roughly chopped

juice of $^1/_2$ lemon

$^1/_4$ cup extra-virgin olive oil, plus extra to drizzle

sea salt and freshly ground black pepper

2 tablespoons chopped flat-leaf parsley

Bring a large saucepan of salted water to the boil and add the spaghetti. Stir well and boil rapidly for 8 minutes, or until al dente.

Meanwhile, combine the crab, chilli, garlic, lemon zest, rocket, lemon juice and olive oil in a small bowl. Season well with sea salt and freshly ground black pepper.

Drain the cooked spaghetti and return it to the pot. Pour over the crab mixture, add the parsley and stir to combine. Drizzle with a little extra olive oil, if desired. Serve immediately.

Serves 2

spaghetti with fresh tomato sauce.

I love the simplicity of this dish – the only cooking required is to boil the spaghetti! You do need good-quality and tasty tomatoes, however, so use vine-ripened varieties, preferably home-grown ones.

500 g (1 lb) tomatoes

2 cloves garlic, very finely chopped

$^1/_4$ cup shredded basil

$^1/_3$ cup extra-virgin olive oil, plus extra, to serve

2 tablespoons balsamic vinegar

salt and freshly ground black pepper

500 g (1 lb) dried spaghetti

freshly grated parmesan, to serve

Though not absolutely necessary, I prefer to peel the tomatoes. To do this, refer to the instructions on page 92.

To make the fresh tomato sauce, halve the tomatoes, remove and discard the seeds and dice the flesh. Place the flesh in a bowl and stir in the garlic, basil, oil and vinegar. Season well with salt and freshly ground black pepper. Allow to stand at room temperature for 1 hour, stirring occasionally.

Bring a large saucepan of salted water to the boil and add the spaghetti. Stir well and boil rapidly until the pasta is al dente.

Drain the cooked pasta and return it to the saucepan. Stir in the sauce. Season to taste with more salt and freshly ground black pepper. Serve spaghetti drizzled with a little extra-virgin olive oil and grated parmesan.

The addition of a little chopped fresh chilli is also delicious.

Serves 4

spaghetti with tuna, rocket and lemon.

This simple dish can be mustered up at a moment's notice and is the perfect pasta for those with not much in the pantry and little time to spare.

250 g (8 oz) dried spaghetti

$^1/_4$ cup roughly chopped rocket (arugula)

grated zest and juice of 1 lemon

2 tablespoons extra-virgin olive oil, plus extra, to serve

1 clove garlic, chopped

$^1/_2$ long red chilli, chopped (optional)

1 × 200 g ($6^1/_2$ oz) can tuna in oil

salt and freshly ground black pepper

Bring a large saucepan of salted water to the boil and add the spaghetti. Stir well and boil rapidly until the pasta is al dente.

Meanwhile, place the rocket, lemon zest and juice, oil, garlic and chilli in a small bowl. Add the tuna along with its oil. Lightly mash the tuna with a fork, then season well with salt and freshly ground black pepper.

Drain the cooked pasta and return it to the saucepan. Stir in the tuna mixture. Drizzle with a little extra oil and serve immediately.

If you have a jar of capers in the refrigerator, add a tablespoonful to the sauce as a variation.

A crisp green salad is the perfect accompaniment to this pasta dish.

Serves 2

spice cake.

1 1/3 cups self-raising (self-rising) flour

seeds from 4 cardamom pods, crushed

1/2 teaspoon mixed spice

salt

3 large eggs, separated

1/2 cup caster (superfine) sugar

grated zest of 1 orange

1/2 cup honey

75 g (2 1/2 oz) butter, melted

1/3 cup strong coffee, freshly made

Preheat the oven to 180°C (350°F, Gas Mark 4). Grease a loaf tin and line the base with baking paper.

Sift the flour, cardamom seeds, mixed spice and a pinch of salt into a bowl.

In a separate bowl, whisk the egg yolks, sugar and zest together for 3–4 minutes, or until pale and fluffy. Add the honey and melted butter and whisk until combined.

Gently fold half the sifted flour into the egg mixture. Lightly stir in the coffee, then fold in the remaining flour.

In a clean, dry bowl, whisk the egg whites with an electric mixer until soft peaks form. Fold the whites through the flour and egg mixture, until combined.

Pour the batter into the prepared loaf tin. Bake for 55–60 minutes, or until golden and firm to the touch. A skewer inserted into the centre should come out clean. Allow to cool in the tin for 10 minutes before turning out onto a wire rack. Serve buttered accompanied with tea or coffee.

Make the cake a day before you want to serve it, as the flavours develop on keeping.

spiced apple sauce.

This sauce is the perfect accompaniment to pork.

2 large cooking apples, peeled, quartered
and cored

2 tablespoons brown sugar

2 cloves

$^1/_2$ teaspoon mixed spice

pinch of ground ginger

Roughly chop the apples and place into a small saucepan with the sugar, spices and 100 ml (3½ fl oz) of water. Cover and cook over low heat, stirring occasionally, for 30 minutes, or until the apples are soft and broken up. During the cooking, add extra water, if needed, to stop the apples from catching on the bottom of the pan.

Mash with a fork or purée the flesh in a small food processor. Taste and adjust the sweetness and spice to suit your palate.

The flesh of a cooking apple quickly cooks down to a fluffy purée, making it perfect for sauces. Bramley apples are a type of cooking apple. They are now being grown in Tasmania and other cooler-climate locations — look for them at growers' markets.

Makes 1 cup

spiced moroccan chicken.

Yoghurt makes an excellent marinade for chicken – here it is combined
with a little spicy harissa.

8 chicken drumsticks

1 tablespoon cornflour (cornstarch)

1 cup plain natural yoghurt

2 tablespoons harissa (see below)

$^1/_3$ cup chopped flat-leaf parsley

$^1/_3$ cup chopped coriander (cilantro) leaves

juice of 1 lemon

chopped flat-leaf parsley, extra, to serve

1 lemon, quartered, to serve

With a sharp knife make a couple of cuts in the thickest part of each drumstick and place chicken in a ceramic or glass dish.

Combine the cornflour, yoghurt, harissa, herbs and lemon juice in a small bowl. Spread the mixture over the chicken pieces and set aside to marinate for 30 minutes.

Preheat the oven to 190°C (375°F, Gas Mark 5).

Place the chicken in a baking tin and cook, turning occasionally, for 35–40 minutes, or until golden and cooked through. Sprinkle with a little extra parsley, garnish with lemon wedges and serve with a green salad.

Harissa, a spicy paste used in Moroccan cooking, is available from good supermarkets and delicatessens. You can make a simple harissa by soaking 5 dried chillies in a little water for 20 minutes. Drain the chillies and place in a blender with 2 peeled garlic cloves, ¼ cup of olive oil, 1 teaspoon of toasted cumin seeds, 2 teaspoons of toasted coriander seeds and a pinch salt. Blend to a thick paste and store, covered with a little extra oil, in a sealed jar in the refrigerator for up to 2 weeks.

Serves 4

spinach soup.

50 g (1³/₄ oz) butter

1 onion, roughly chopped

1 leek, sliced

500 g (1 lb) fresh or frozen spinach

3 medium-sized potatoes, peeled and
    roughly chopped

1 bay leaf

1.25 litres (40 fl oz) chicken or vegetable
    stock

2 tablespoons cream

pinch of freshly grated nutmeg

salt and freshly ground black pepper

juice of ¹/₂ lemon

2 tablespoons chopped chives

Heat the butter over moderate heat in a large saucepan. Add the onion and leek and cook, stirring occasionally, for 4–5 minutes, or until the vegetables are soft but not coloured. Add the spinach and potatoes and cook for 2–3 minutes. Add the bay leaf and stock and bring to the boil. Reduce the heat and simmer for 30 minutes.

Remove from the heat and allow to cool a little. Discard the bay leaf. Purée the soup in batches in a blender or with a hand-held blender until smooth. Stir in the cream and nutmeg, then return the soup to the heat but don't let it boil. Season to taste with salt and freshly ground black pepper and lemon juice. Serve hot or cold, garnished with chives.

I like to accompany this soup with bits of crisp bacon or prosciutto and toast.

Serves 4

steak sandwich.

1 × 150 g (5 oz) rump, chuck, New-York cut
   or sirloin steak
olive oil
salt and freshly ground black pepper
1 small baguette, Turkish bread or ciabatta

knob of butter
Dijon mustard
small handful of rocket (arugula)
2 slices ripe tomato

Dry the piece of steak with kitchen paper, then flatten it to a thickness of about 5 mm (¼ in) by hitting it with a rolling pin or mallet, or with your fist.

Heat a heavy grill pan or frying pan to very hot. Brush the steak with a little oil and season well with salt and freshly ground black pepper. Add the steak to the pan and cook for about 1–2 minutes each side – this will give you a medium-done steak. Allow a little more or less cooking time depending on your taste.

Transfer the steak to a plate and let it rest, covered with foil, for about 5 minutes, turning it occasionally to coat it in its own meat juices.

Slice the baguette in half and spread it with a little butter and some Dijon mustard. Place the steak on the bottom half of the bread. Top with a handful of rocket and the slices of tomato. Drizzle with any meat juice from the resting plate and season well with more salt and freshly ground pepper. Top with the remaining bread and serve immediately.

Letting the steak rest after cooking allows the meat to relax, making it tender.

Use your favourite type of bread – I often make a steak sandwich with thick slices of good white Italian-style bread.

Serves 1

stuffed dates.

Plump fresh dates, with their sweet, sticky flesh, are ideal for stuffing. In this recipe, the bitter orange from the marmalade nicely balances out the sweetness of the fruit and chocolate.

12 fresh dates	**12 whole blanched almonds**
3 tablespoons orange marmalade	**110 g (3^1/$_2$ oz) white chocolate**

Make a slit in the side of each date and remove the stone.

Carefully spoon about a teaspoon of the marmalade into each date, being careful not to over-fill them. Insert a blanched almond into each slit.

Break the white chocolate into squares and melt it in a heatproof bowl set over a saucepan of hot water, stirring occasionally, until smooth. Remove the bowl from the heat and allow the chocolate to cool slightly. Dip half of each date into the chocolate, then leave to set on a wire rack.

Stuffed dates are delicious served with coffee at the end of dinner.

Makes 12

stuffed peaches.

4 ripe slipstone peaches

8 amaretti biscuits, crushed

30 g (1 oz) butter, chilled and chopped

2 tablespoons demerera sugar or raw sugar, plus extra to sprinkle

2 tablespoons flaked almonds

Preheat the oven to 180°C (350°F, Gas Mark 4). Peel the peaches, if desired, then cut in half and remove the stones.

Roughly combine the crushed biscuits, butter, sugar and flaked almonds.

Place the peach halves close together in a baking tin. Spoon an equal amount of the biscuit mixture into the centre of each peach half. Sprinkle with a little extra sugar.

Bake for 15 minutes, or until the peaches are tender and the biscuit mixture is crisp. Serve with vanilla ice-cream.

Amaretti are little crisp Italian biscuits, flavoured with almond. They are available from most large supermarkets and delicatessens.

Serves 4

summer pudding.

**1 kg (2 lb) mixed berries (use a
combination of raspberries,
blackberries, blueberries, redcurrants
or blackcurrants)**

**²/₃ cup caster (superfine) sugar
10 thin slices stale white bread, crusts
removed**

Place the berries, sugar and ¼ cup of water in a saucepan. Bring to a gentle simmer over low heat and cook, stirring to dissolve the sugar, for about 3 minutes, or until the fruit has softened and produced lots of juice. Set aside to cool.

Pour the juice into a flat dish, reserving the fruit.

Cut one slice of bread into a circle small enough to fit the base of a 1.5 litre (48 fl oz) pudding basin, and another large enough to fit the top. Cut the remaining slices into triangles.

Dip both sides of the smaller circle of bread quickly into the juice and place it in the bottom of the basin. Dip both sides of each triangle of bread into the juice, then place around the inside of the basin, overlapping them slightly to make sure there are no gaps. Store any remaining juice in the refrigerator, to serve with the pudding.

Fill the basin with berries and cover with the larger circle of bread, trimming it if necessary. Cover the top of the pudding with plastic wrap and press in a saucer or small plate that just fits inside the rim of the basin. Weigh down the plate with a heavy can or two. Place the basin in a shallow dish to catch any juice that might overflow, and refrigerate for at least 12 hours.

To serve, run a thin knife around the inside of the bowl and invert the pudding onto a serving plate. Cut into wedges and serve accompanied with thick cream and any reserved juice.

Serves 8

sweetcorn and chicken soup.

1.75 litres (55 fl oz) chicken or vegetable
   stock
3 cobs of corn
1 tablespoon cornflour (cornstarch)
150 ml ($4^{1}/_{2}$ fl oz) cream

2 tablespoons dry sherry
2 skinless chicken breasts, finely chopped
salt and freshly ground black pepper
2 tablespoons shredded spring onions
   (scallions)

Bring the stock to the boil in a large saucepan. Add the corn and simmer for 8–10 minutes, or until tender.

Remove the corn from the saucepan, leaving the cooking water in the pan.

Allow the corn to cool enough to handle, then, using a sharp knife, cut the kernels from the cobs.

Place half the kernels back into the saucepan with the reserved cooking liquid. Place the remaining kernels with the cornflour and cream in a food processor and purée until smooth. Transfer to the saucepan and bring to a gentle simmer over medium heat, stirring frequently. Add the sherry and chicken. Stir over medium heat for 5–10 minutes, or until the chicken is cooked. Season to taste with salt and lots of freshly ground black pepper. Serve garnished with the shredded spring onions.

A nice touch is to add a dash of soy sauce to the soup just before serving. It is also good with a drizzle of sesame oil in each bowl.

Serves 4

swiss roll.

4 eggs

$^1/_2$ cup caster (superfine) sugar

1 teaspoon vanilla essence

$^2/_3$ cup plain (all-purpose) flour

50 g ($1^3/_4$ oz) ground almonds (almond meal)

1 teaspoon baking powder

caster (superfine) sugar, extra, to sprinkle

$^1/_3$ cup raspberry jam

Preheat the oven to 200°C (400°F, Gas Mark 6). Grease a 20 × 30 cm (8 × 12 in) Swiss roll tin and line the base with baking paper, leaving a little paper overhanging along the two long sides.

Combine the eggs, sugar and vanilla in a large mixing bowl. Whisk with a hand-held electric mixer for 3–4 minutes, or until the mixture is frothy and pale and has increased in volume – the beaters should leave a trail when lifted out of the mixture.

Sift the flour into the bowl and add the ground almonds and baking powder. Using a large metal spoon, gently fold the dry ingredients into the egg mixture until just combined.

Pour the mixture into the prepared tin and tap the tin gently to distribute the batter into the corners. Bake for 10–15 minutes, or until golden and firm to the touch – the cake should have just begun to shrink from the edges of the tin.

Using the overhanging baking paper, turn the cake out onto a piece of baking paper that has been generously sprinkled with caster sugar. Peel off the baking paper from the cooked cake. With the help of the sugared baking paper, roll up the cake from the short end. Let the roll sit for 10 minutes, then unroll it. Trim the edges of the cake and spread evenly with the jam, then re-roll. Transfer to a serving plate.

It is important to fold in the flour and almonds very gently. If you are too vigorous at this stage, you will lose a lot of the volume in the egg mixture.

terrine.

500 g (1 lb) rashers streaky bacon	100 g ($3^{1}/_{2}$ oz) pistachio nuts
25 g ($^{3}/_{4}$ oz) butter	$^{1}/_{3}$ cup brandy
1 onion, chopped	2 tablespoons chopped rosemary
2 cloves garlic, chopped	2 tablespoons chopped thyme
750 g ($1^{1}/_{2}$ lb) minced (ground) pork	2 tablespoons snipped fresh chives
350 g (11 oz) rindless boned pork belly, finely chopped	6 juniper berries, crushed
	2 teaspoons salt
250 g (8 oz) chicken livers, finely chopped	$1^{1}/_{2}$ teaspoons freshly ground black pepper

Preheat the oven to 170°C (340°F, Gas Mark 3). Lightly grease a 1.5 litre (48 fl oz) terrine or loaf tin. Line the tin horizontally with three quarters of the bacon rashers, overlapping each rasher slightly and leaving 5 cm overhanging the tin.

Melt the butter in a frying pan over low heat. Add the onion and garlic and cook until soft and just coloured. Transfer to a large bowl. Chop the remaining bacon and add it to the onion mixture. Add the remaining ingredients and mix well.

Spoon the mixture into the prepared terrine dish, pushing the mixture down and levelling the top. Fold over the overlapping bacon. Cover the dish with a lid or with foil and place in a deep baking tin. Pour enough boiling water into the baking tin to come halfway up the side of the terrine. Bake for 1½ hours.

Remove the terrine dish from the baking tin and allow to cool.

Meanwhile, cut out a piece of cardboard that fits the inside rim of the dish and cover it with foil. Place it on top of the terrine and place a few unopened cans on top. Weigh down the terrine overnight in the refrigerator.

Turn the terrine out of the dish and thickly slice. Serve with bread and chutney.

Serves 10–12

thai green curry paste.

8 long green chillies, seeded and sliced

1 small onion or shallot, roughly chopped

5 cloves garlic, peeled and roughly
   chopped

1 large handful coriander (cilantro), stems
   and leaves

2 stems lemongrass, lower part of stem
   crushed and sliced

1 × 5 cm (2 in) piece fresh ginger, peeled
   and roughly chopped

3 kaffir lime leaves, shredded

2 teaspoons coriander seeds

1 teaspoon cumin seeds

1 teaspoon sea salt

1 teaspoon freshly ground black pepper

1 tablespoon Thai fish sauce

2–3 tablespoons sunflower or peanut oil

Place the chilli, onion, garlic, coriander stems and leaves, lemongrass, ginger, kaffir lime leaves, coriander seeds, cumin seeds, salt, pepper and fish sauce into a food processor or blender. Add 1 tablespoon of the oil and process. With the machine still running, pour in enough extra oil in a thin stream for the mixture to form a smooth paste. Store, covered with a little extra oil, in a screw-top jar in the refrigerator for up to 1 month.

Makes about 1 cup

thai-style chicken salad.

3 skinless chicken breasts

1 tablespoon peanut oil

salt and freshly ground black pepper

$^{1}/_{3}$ cup raw unsalted peanuts

100 g ($3^{1}/_{2}$ oz) rice vermicelli (cellophane) noodles

1 Lebanese cucumber, peeled and diced

250 g (8 oz) mixed salad leaves

1 cup coriander (cilantro) sprigs

DRESSING

2 tablespoons Thai fish sauce

2 tablespoons lime juice

1 tablespoon soy sauce

1 teaspoon peanut oil

2 small red chillies, seeded and finely chopped

2 teaspoons brown sugar or palm sugar

Flatten the chicken breasts to a thickness of about 5 mm (¼ in) by hitting them with a rolling pin or mallet, or with your fist.

Heat a large frying pan over high heat. Brush each breast with a little oil and season well with salt and freshly ground black pepper. Place in the pan and cook for 3–4 minutes each side, or until cooked. Remove from the pan and set aside. Add the peanuts to the pan and cook, stirring, until golden. Set aside.

Place the noodles in a heatproof bowl and cover with boiling water. Leave for 6–7 minutes, or until soft. Drain well and cut into 3 cm (1¼ in) lengths.

Place the dressing ingredients in a screw-top jar and shake well to combine.

Slice the chicken into 1 cm (½ in) strips.

To serve, mix together the cucumber, salad leaves, coriander sprigs and noodles and place on a large platter or in a large bowl. Top with the chicken. Pour over the dressing and scatter with the peanuts.

Serves 4

tiramisu.

3 eggs, separated

$^1/_3$ cup caster (superfine) sugar

300 ml (9$^1/_2$ fl oz) mascarpone

1$^1/_2$ cups strong black coffee, at room
temperature

$^1/_4$ cup brandy or coffee-flavoured liqueur

16–20 Savoiardi biscuits

100 g (3$^1/_2$ oz) dark chocolate, grated

1 tablespoon cocoa, sifted

Beat the egg yolks and sugar together in a bowl with a hand-held beater or whisk for 3 minutes, or until pale and thick. Gradually fold in the mascarpone.

Using a clean, dry bowl, whisk the egg whites with clean beaters until stiff peaks form. Fold the whites into the mascarpone mixture.

Mix together the coffee and brandy and pour into a flat-bottomed bowl. Using eight of the Savoiardi biscuits, dip each one into the coffee for a few seconds. They will rapidly absorb the coffee, so only a very quick dip is needed. Do not let them become soggy. Line the base of a 1-litre capacity deep ceramic dish with the biscuits – they should sit evenly next to each other. Use a few extra biscuits if your dish is larger.

Cover the biscuits with half the mascarpone mixture. Repeat with a layer of coffee-soaked biscuits and cover with the remaining mascarpone. Cover with plastic wrap and refrigerate for at least 4 hours.

Just before serving, combine the grated chocolate and cocoa and sprinkle over the tiramisu.

Savoiardi or sponge-finger biscuits are dry, light, finger-shaped biscuits. They are available from larger supermarkets and delicatessens.

Tiramisu is also good made in a large glass bowl – a bit like a trifle.

Serves 6

tuna pâté.

2 × 200 g (6¹/₂ oz) cans tuna in oil, drained
75 g (2¹/₂ oz) butter, softened
125 g (4 oz) cream cheese, softened
juice of 1 lemon

¹/₄ cup snipped fresh chives
2 tablespoons chopped parsley
1 teaspoon Dijon mustard
sea salt and freshly ground black pepper

Place all the ingredients except the salt and pepper in a food processor and, using the pulse action, process the mixture in short bursts until just combined. Season well with sea salt and freshly ground black pepper. Taste and add extra lemon juice, if desired. Serve with crusty bread or crackers.

Makes about 1 cup

vegetarian lasagne.

2 tablespoons olive oil

250 g (8 oz) cherry tomatoes, halved

2 cloves garlic, crushed

3 × 400 g (13 oz) cans crushed tomatoes

salt and freshly ground black pepper

$^1/_2$ cup roughly torn basil leaves

500 g (1 lb) ricotta

2 eggs, lightly beaten

$^1/_2$ cup cream

pinch of ground nutmeg

1 cup coarsely grated parmesan

450 g (14 oz) button mushrooms, sliced

150 g (5 oz) baby English spinach leaves

10–12 sheets dried lasagne

1 cup grated mozzarella

Heat half the oil in a large saucepan over medium heat. Add the cherry tomatoes, garlic and crushed tomatoes and simmer for 30 minutes. Season, add the basil and set aside.

In a bowl, combine the ricotta, eggs, cream, nutmeg and half the parmesan.

Heat the remaining oil in a large saucepan and sauté the mushrooms for 5–6 minutes. Add the spinach and cook for 1–2 minutes, or until the spinach has just softened. Set aside.

Cook the lasagne sheets, two at a time, in a large saucepan of boiling salted water for 30 seconds. Remove and refresh by placing in a bowl of iced water for 2 minutes. Drain well on a clean tea towel.

Preheat the oven to 180°C (350°F, Gas Mark 4). Grease a 25.5 × 18 × 5 cm (10 × 7 × 2 in) ceramic lasagne dish.

Line the dish with a layer of pasta. Cover with half of the tomato sauce and top with half of the mozzarella. Cover with another layer of pasta, then spread over the mushroom mixture and top with half the ricotta mixture. Add another layer of pasta, then the remaining tomato sauce, mozzarella, ricotta and remaining parmesan, seasoning each layer. Bake for 1 hour, or until golden. Leave to rest for 10 minutes before serving.

Serves 6

victoria sponge.

A perfectly made Victoria sponge is a fine thing indeed. This recipe is from British writer Katie Stewart, whose recipes are not only delicious and reliable, but always inspired and generous with information. I return time and time again to her *Times* cookbook (now sadly out of print).

175 g (6 oz) unsalted butter, softened
175 g (6 oz) caster (superfine) sugar
3 large eggs, at room temperature
$^1/_2$ teaspoon vanilla essence
175 g (6 oz) self-raising (self-rising) flour, sifted

3–4 tablespoons fruit jam (apricot, raspberry, strawberry or plum), to fill
icing (confectioners') sugar, to dust

Preheat the oven to 180°C (350°F, Gas Mark 4). Grease two 19 cm (7½ in) shallow round cake tins and line the base of each with baking paper.

In a bowl, beat the butter and sugar with a hand-held electric beater until pale and fluffy – about 8 minutes.

In a separate bowl, beat the eggs and vanilla with a fork. Add the egg mixture to the butter mixture a little at a time, beating well with the electric beater after each addition. Towards the end, if the mixture looks like it is separating, add a little of the flour with the last amount of egg.

Using a large metal spoon, gently fold in half the flour. Fold in the remaining flour until combined – the mixture should drop from the spoon if given a slight shake. Spoon the mixture evenly into the prepared tins and level the tops. Bake for 20–25 minutes, or until golden and springy to the touch. Allow to cool in the tins for 2 minutes, then turn out onto a wire rack to cool completely.

Spread the jam evenly over one of the cakes, then top with the remaining cake. Dust with icing sugar.

yoghurt cheese.

This is a simple soft cheese with a lovely creamy texture – a little like cream cheese – which can be easily made at home. Yoghurt gives it a nice tang.

1 litre (32 fl oz) plain natural yoghurt | **1 teaspoon salt**

Line a sieve or colander with a large square of damp muslin. Stir the salt into the yoghurt and pour the yoghurt into the lined sieve. Tie the muslin with string to form a bag, then hang the yoghurt from a shelf in the refrigerator, placing a bowl underneath to catch the draining liquid. Leave for 24–48 hours.

Remove from the refrigerator and roll the cheese into walnut-sized balls. Store in the refrigerator and eat within a couple of days.

Adding herbs to the finished cheese is a delicious variation. Stir in 1–2 tablespoons of chives, basil or parsley and some extra salt or pepper if needed.

Yoghurt cheese is delicious served alongside fresh or poached fruit. Leave out the salt from the original mixture and serve sweetened with a little sugar or honey.

To store the cheese for a week or so, transfer the balls to a screw-top jar and pour over enough olive oil to cover. You can add a sprig of rosemary, some chopped herbs or 1 crushed clove of garlic to the jar to flavour the cheese, if desired.

Makes 8–10 balls

yoghurt cream.

I make this simple dessert more than any other – the results are delicious and the
effort is minimal. It can be served either as an accompaniment to fruit (both fresh
and cooked), or as part of a topping for fresh fruit. It is best made at least
3 hours in advance to allow the sugar to 'melt'.

300 ml (9^1/$_2$ fl oz) cream
100 ml (3^1/$_2$ fl oz) plain natural yoghurt

^{1}/$_2$ cup lightly packed brown sugar

Pour the cream into a medium-sized bowl and beat with a whisk or hand-held electric
mixer until it forms soft peaks. Stir through the yoghurt. Transfer to a 3-cup capacity
deep dish (the cream should be at least 5 cm (2 in) deep) and smooth the surface.

Sprinkle the top with an even layer of brown sugar, covering the yoghurt cream
completely – this may take a little extra sugar, depending on the size of the dish.

Place in the refrigerator for 3–4 hours. You will end up with a softly set yoghurt and
cream mixture with a runny 'caramel' topping.

Yoghurt cream is delicious served with grilled peaches.

*I make a 'cheat's fruit brûlée' by putting a layer of fruit (berries or freshly sliced mango work
well) in the base of the dish before adding the yoghurt cream and brown sugar.*

The cream is also delicious flavoured with a little vanilla.

zabaglione.

Zabaglione is an Italian-style custard made with egg yolks, sugar and marsala. It is
usually eaten warm from small glasses and is delicious accompanied with thin,
sweet biscuits, sponge fingers or sprinkled with crumbled amaretti biscuits

4 eggs

$^1/_3$ cup caster (superfine) sugar

grated zest of $^1/_2$ lemon

100 ml ($3^1/_2$ oz) marsala

Place the eggs, sugar and lemon zest in a bowl. Whisk by hand (if you are feeling strong)
or with a hand-held electric beater until pale and frothy.

Place the bowl over a saucepan half-filled with hot water – make sure the bowl
doesn't touch the water. Place the saucepan over low heat. Slowly whisk in the marsala,
then continue to whisk for a further 5 minutes, or until the mixture is warm, frothy,
mousse-like and doubled in volume. Be careful that the mixture doesn't boil or it will
curdle and the eggs will start to scramble. If it is becoming too hot, remove from the
heat for a moment and continue to whisk until it cools slightly.

Serve warm in small glasses.

*Marsala is a sweet fortified wine made in Sicily. It is traditional to use marsala for zabaglione,
but a sweet dessert wine can be used instead.*

Zabaglione is delicious poured over sliced ripe strawberries, berries or peaches.

Zabaglione can also be chilled for several hours and served cold.

Serves 4

conversions.

All cup and spoon measurements are level.

I use 60 g (2 oz, grade 3) eggs.

All recipes were tested using a regular convection oven. If you are using a fan-forced oven, set your oven temperature to approximately 20°C (70°F) lower than is recommended in the recipe.

Cup conversions

1 cup uncooked arborio rice = 220 g (7 oz)
1 cup uncooked basmati/long-grain rice = 200 g
   (6 ½ oz)
1 cup sugar = 250 g (8 oz)
1 cup brown sugar = 185 g (6 oz)
1 cup caster (superfine) sugar = 250 g (8 oz)
1 cup icing (confectioners') sugar = 250 g (8 oz)
1 cup fresh breadcrumbs = 80 g (2 ½ oz)
1 cup plain or self-raising (self-rising) flour = 150g
   (5 oz)
1 cup cornflour (cornstarch) = 150 g (5 oz)
1 cup grated cheddar = 125 g (4 oz)
1 cup grated mozzarella = 150 g (5 oz)
1 cup grated parmesan = 100 g (3 ½ oz)

Liquid conversions

metric	imperial	standard cups
30 ml	1 fl oz	2 tablespoons
60 ml	2 fl oz	¼ cup
80 ml	2 ¾ fl oz	⅓ cup
125 ml	4 fl oz	½ cup
185 ml	6 fl oz	¾ cup
250 ml	8 fl oz	1 cup

Dry measurements

metric	imperial
15 g	½ oz
30 g	1 oz
45 g	1 ½ oz
55 g	2 oz
125 g	4 oz
150 g	5 oz
200 g	6 ½ oz
225 g	7 oz
250 g	8 oz
500 g	1 lb
1 kg	2 lb

Oven temperatures

Celcius	Fahrenheit	Gas Mark
120°C very slow	250°F	1
150°C slow	300°F	2
160°C warm	315°F	2–3
180°C moderate	350°F	4
190°C moderately hot	375°F	5
200°C moderately hot	400°F	6
220°C hot	425°F	7
230°C very hot	450°F	8
240°C very hot	475°F	9

index.

affogato 2

almond bread 4

apples

    apple and cinnamon teacake 5

    apple tart 6

    braised pork chops with apple 17

    spiced apple sauce 149

apricot turnovers 8

asparagus 9

asparagus risotto 10

baked ricotta 12

banana smoothie 13

barbecue sauce 14

beef

    beef and mushroom pie 16

    hamburgers 68

    steak sandwich 153

beetroot, roast 130

berries

    free-form blueberry pie 58

    fruit tart 61

    raspberry cordial 125

    raspberry sundae 126

    summer pudding 158

biscuits

    chocolate chip cookies 33

    orange biscuits 96

    peanut biscuits 108

braised pork chops with apple 17

breads

    bruschetta 18

damper 50

    focaccia 56

bruschetta 18

butter, maître d'hôtel 84

cakes

    apple and cinnamon teacake 5

    chocolate peanut butter cake 37

    madeleines 82

    orange poppy seed cake 98

    orange semolina cake 99

    spice cake 148

    swiss roll 161

    victoria sponge 170

    see also slices

carrot salad 20

cheese

    baked ricotta 12

    cheese and chive dumplings 52

    feta, cheddar and chive muffins 54

    macaroni cheese 81

    yoghurt cheese 172

cherries, poached 114

chicken

    chicken cacciatore 22

    chicken casserole with peas and

        pancetta 23

    chicken, lemon and rocket risotto 24

    chicken liver pâté 26

    chicken pot roast 28

    chinese-style braised chicken 32

    lemon chicken 77

portuguese chicken 110

spiced moroccan chicken 150

sweetcorn and chicken soup 160

thai-style chicken salad 165

chilli

chilli oil 30

chilli sauce 31

piri piri sauce 110

spaghetti with crab and chilli 144

chinese-style braised chicken 32

chocolate

chocolate chip cookies 33

chocolate fondant puddings 34

chocolate icing 36

chocolate macaroons 35

chocolate muffins 36

chocolate peanut butter cake 37

cocoa 40

mocha 90

tiramisu 166

christmas pudding 38

cocktail sauce 119

cocoa 40

coffee

affogato 2

mocha 90

tiramisu 166

cordial

orange 97

raspberry 125

corn *see* sweetcorn

corned beef (silverside) 42

cream, yoghurt 173

creamed corn 43

crème brûlée 44

crêpes with lemon and sugar 45

curries

curry powder 46

green fish curry 65

quick indian-style lamb curry 124

thai green curry paste 164

custard 48

damper 50

dates, stuffed 154

dipping sauce 60

dressing, mustard 62

drinks

banana smoothie 13

cocoa 40

mocha 90

orange cordial 97

raspberry cordial 125

dumplings 52

eggplant parmigiano 53

feta, cheddar and chive muffins 54

fish

fish lasagne 55

gravlax 62

green fish curry 65

kedgeree 72

roast fish in paper 131

salade niçoise 134

spaghetti with tuna, rocket and lemon 147

tuna pâté 167

focaccia 56

free-form blueberry pie 58
fresh spring rolls 60
fruit tart 61

gravlax 62
greek salad 64
green fish curry 65
grilled peaches 66

hamburgers 68
harissa 150
hazelnut slice 69
honeycomb 70

ice-cream
    affogato 2
    hokey-pokey ice-cream 70
    lemon ice-cream 78
    passionfruit ice-cream 100
    raspberry sundae 126
icing, chocolate 36

kedgeree 72

laksa 73
lamb
    lamb shanks 74
    quick indian-style lamb curry 124
    slow-roasted lamb 141
lemon
    chicken, lemon and rocket risotto 24
    lemon bars 76
    lemon chicken 77
    lemon ice-cream 78

lemon posset 80
    spaghetti with tuna, rocket and lemon 147

macaroni cheese 81
madeleines 82
maître d'hôtel butter 84
mango sorbet 86
marmalade 87
    onion marmalade 94
mayonnaise, mustard 42
meat loaf 88
meringues 89
    chocolate macaroons 35
mocha 90
muffins
    chocolate muffins 36
    feta, cheddar and chive muffins 54
mushroom and beef pie 16
mussel broth 92
mustard dressing 62
mustard mayonnaise 42

noodles
    laksa 73
    singapore-style noodles 140

oil, chilli 30
onion marmalade 94
orange biscuits 96
orange cordial 97
orange poppy seed cake 98
orange semolina cake 99
orange syrup 98

passionfruit ice-cream 100
passionfruit syllabub 102
pasta
 fish lasagne 55
 fresh pasta 103
 macaroni cheese 81
 pasta with zucchini 104
 spaghetti vongole 143
 spaghetti with crab and chilli 144
 spaghetti with fresh tomato sauce 146
 spaghetti with tuna, rocket and lemon 147
 vegetarian lasagne 168
pastry
 quick flaky pastry 122
 shortcrust pastry 106
pâté
 chicken liver pâté 26
 tuna pâté 167
peaches
 grilled peaches 66
 peach pie 106
 stuffed peaches 156
peanut biscuits 108
pears, roast 132
pies
 beef and mushroom pie 16
 free-form blueberry pie 58
 peach pie 106
piri piri sauce 110
pizza
 basic dough 111
 pizza bianca 111
 pizza margherita 112
 tomato sauce 112

poached cherries 114
pommes anna 115
pork
 braised pork chops with apple 17
 meat loaf 88
 pork satays 116
 san choy bow 136
 slow-roasted pork 142
 terrine 162
portuguese chicken 110
portuguese custard tarts 118
potatoes
 pommes anna 115
prawns
 prawn cocktail 119
 prawn toasts 120
 salt-baked prawns 135
puddings
 chocolate fondant puddings 34
 christmas pudding 38
 lemon posset 80
 summer pudding 158
 tiramisu 166

quiche lorraine 121
quick flaky pastry 122
quick indian-style lamb curry 124

raspberry cordial 125
raspberry sundae 126
rice
 asparagus risotto 10
 chicken, lemon and rocket risotto 24
 kedgeree 72

risotto with sausage and red wine 128
roast beetroot 130
roast fish in paper 131
roast pears 132
rosemary focaccia 56

salads
    carrot salad 20
    greek salad 64
    salade niçoise 134
    thai-style chicken salad 165
salt-baked prawns 135
san choy bow 136
sandwich, steak 153
satays, pork 116
sauces
    barbecue sauce 14
    chilli sauce 31
    cocktail sauce 119
    dipping sauce 60
    fresh tomato sauce 146
    piri piri sauce 110
    satay sauce 138
    spiced apple sauce 149
    tomato pizza sauce 112
sausages
    risotto with sausage and red wine 128
    sausage roast 139
seafood
    mussel broth 92
    prawn cocktail 119
    prawn toasts 120
    salt-baked prawns 135
    spaghetti vongole 143

spaghetti with crab and chilli 144
shortcrust pastry 106
silverside (corned beef) 42
singapore-style noodles 140
slices
    hazelnut slice 69
    lemon bars 76
slow-roasted lamb 141
slow-roasted pork 142
smoothie, banana 13
sorbet, mango 86
soups
    spinach soup 152
    sweetcorn and chicken soup 160
spaghetti vongole 143
spaghetti with crab and chilli 144
spaghetti with fresh tomato sauce 146
spaghetti with tuna, rocket and lemon 147
spice cake 148
spiced apple sauce 149
spiced moroccan chicken 150
spinach soup 152
spring rolls, fresh 60
steak sandwich 153
strawberry fruit tart 61
stuffed dates 154
stuffed peaches 156
summer pudding 158
sweetcorn
    creamed corn 43
    sweetcorn and chicken soup 160
swiss roll 161
syllabub, passionfruit 102